W9-AUX-458

Spiritual Plateaus

Spiritual Plateaus

Glenn L. Pace

Deseret Book Company
Salt Lake City, Utah

Library of Congress Cataloging-in-Publication Data

Pace, Glenn L.
    Spiritual plateaus / Glenn L. Pace.
      p.   cm.
    Includes bibliographical references and index.
    ISBN 0-87579-337-1 (hard)
    1. Christian life—Mormon authors.   I. Title.
BX8656.P28   1991
248.4'89332—dc20   90-22973
                                                       CIP

Printed in the United States of America

10   9   8   7   6   5   4   3   2   1

Contents

Preface

On the Sunday afternoon of April 7, 1985, as a newly called General Authority, I stood petrified at the pulpit in the Salt Lake Tabernacle. I had received my call forty-eight hours earlier and had completed my talk forty-eight seconds earlier. Among more important things, I said:

"Several years ago, I made a covenant with the Lord. I promised to give him anything he should require of me, and prayed this gesture might warrant forgiveness of my transgressions. Yesterday I gave the only thing I had left. It was something I cherished. I held onto it until the very last moment. I never thought of it as a selfish possession. That of which I speak flew out the window of my home when I turned on the television to watch the news and saw my picture on the television screen. I speak of my prized remaining possession — anonymity.

"How I love not to be noticed! I don't want to sit with the General Authorities in the 'fishbowl' at the BYU football games in my dark blue suit! I want to sit in the stands with my father, wearing an obnoxious T-shirt that reads: 'BYU #1. Enough said!' I have license and credentials to be obnoxious! I was born and raised in Provo, Utah. I attended school at Provo High School. I received my bachelor's and master's degrees from BYU. I'm a member of the Church, and I even work for the Church. My credentials are impeccable. I want to go berserk in the upper tier of the San Diego Stadium as I have the last four years at the Holiday Bowl—with the exception of Ohio State (which soundly beat BYU's team in the bowl game), when I went into deep depression. . . . Nevertheless, I give up my prized anonymity, just as I will give up my life if it is required of me. . . .

"I express my deepest loyalty to Bishop [Robert D.] Hales and his First Counselor, Bishop [Henry B.] Eyring. I will not betray their trust. I express my love and loyalty to the First Presidency, the Council of the Twelve Apostles, the First Quorum of the Seventy, and those I love most— the rank-and-file members of the Church.

"I thank God I was born of goodly parents. I begged my mother not to stand and take my picture as I came to the stand for the first time yesterday morning! But what would I have done if, during my formative years, she had not demonstrated that same pride and enthusiasm for everything I accomplished, however small. My father, Bishop Kenneth L. Pace, was the bishop of the Bonneville Ward in the East Provo Stake during my teens. He remains uppermost in my mind as exemplifying the pure love of Christ throughout his life." (Conference Report, April 1985, pp. 100–101.)

I was not prepared for the response that moment of

complete honesty would bring from the average member of the Church. I love to communicate with the "common folks" because that is who I am, and it is such Saints for whom I have a special love.

This book is dedicated to the rank-and-file members of the Church, the majority of whom have not been a bishop, stake president, Relief Society president, Primary president, Young Women president, regional representative, mission president, or temple president or matron. I personally had never served in any of those positions when I was set apart as second counselor in the Presiding Bishopric. However, I, like you, have a great love for our Heavenly Father, for the Savior, for the gospel, for the Brethren, and for all of my brothers and sisters in the gospel who are out there in the trenches slugging it out with the adversary and dealing with the challenges of life.

Over the past few years, as I have visited informally with the Saints in places ranging from stake conferences to shopping malls, I have recognized two common problems. The first has to do with a lack of spiritual self-confidence. I hear many beautiful testimonies immediately followed by, "I'm not doing too well. I'm not sure I can make it."

The second is closely related and sometimes springs forth from a lack of self-confidence. When people doubt they can make it, rather than going faster they begin to coast. As I meet with stake presidencies prior to stake conferences, I always ask, "What is the biggest problem facing your stake?" The answer in many cases is, "Apathy and lack of commitment." I am convinced that one big reason for such apathy is a lack of self-confidence and a lack of vision as to one's own spiritual potential.

The objective of this "love letter to the Saints" is to awaken each individual to his or her spiritual potential. The spiritual plateaus described in this book are available to every Latter-day Saint who lives the laws upon which the blessings are predicated. These blessings have absolutely nothing to do with a person's position in the Church, but everything to do with a person's purity in the gospel.

Introduction

In April 1979, President Spencer W. Kimball said: "This impression weighs upon me—that the Church is at a point in its growth and maturity when we are at last ready to move forward in a major way. . . . The basic decisions needed for us to move forward, as a people, must be made by the individual members of the Church. The major strides which must be made by the Church will follow upon the major strides to be made by us as individuals. We have paused on some plateaus long enough. Let us resume our journey forward and upward." (Conference Report, April 1979, p. 114.)

Think back to 1979. How old were you? Where were you living? How many children, or brothers and sisters, did you have? What grade in school were you in, or where were you employed? Once you have set a benchmark in your life, see if you can remember where you were spiritually, especially as it compares to your spirituality today.

President Kimball told us we had paused on some plateaus long enough. Have you moved on to a higher spiritual plateau? Are you still stuck on the same one? Perhaps you've fallen off a cliff and at the present moment see no way back.

Our family has a tradition of taking an annual hike to the top of Mount Timpanogos, a high peak north of Provo, Utah. We divide the hike into three segments. Our first plateau is at about five miles. All along the trail we see beautiful wildflowers, but at the end of five miles is a huge bowl where the flowers are brilliant. There we eat a snack and lie down to rest. While resting there we can look up to a higher plateau and see what we call the "saddle," which is over two miles away. Because the trail there is above the timberline, we can see other hikers laboring upward, and we are tempted to stay in our present comfort zone. The trail ahead of us is steeper, we'll have to cross some snowfields, and the air is becoming thinner as we climb toward that 10,000-foot level.

However, our goal is to make it to the top, and after a reasonable rest, we find the energy required to make it to the second plateau, the "saddle." There, a steady, cool breeze greets us, and for the first time on the hike we can see out over Utah Valley and Utah Lake to the west, the Salt Lake Valley to the north, Kennecott's open-pit copper mine in the mountains to the northwest, and Mount Nebo many miles to the south. While for some time it has been hard to breathe in the thin air, now we feel refreshed and exhilarated. We can look back at the beautiful bowl filled with flowers and say, "We made it this far, and it was worth the effort."

From this resting place, we can see that the final plateau

is about a mile away at the 12,000-foot altitude. From where we are sitting, it looks like it is straight up. Our muscles tighten, our eyelids become heavy, and our resolve to put forth more effort wanes as we contemplate what lies ahead. However, our goal is the top of that peak, which means we'll have to leave the comfort zone once more to move on to the highest plateau.

Our goal here in mortality is to keep our second estate and return to the presence of our Father in Heaven. The gospel has been restored to the earth to provide all that is needed to accomplish that objective. I don't know what spiritual plateaus President Kimball had in mind, but I would like to suggest three. Let me hasten to say that this is merely one way of looking at our spiritual development, and not the only way of looking at it. Any one of the plateaus I suggest might be broken down into many parts, and there might be hundreds of plateaus along the way, but for the purposes of this discussion, I have tried to keep the analogy simple.

The three plateaus I would like to suggest are (1) testimony, (2) sanctification, and (3) spiritual graduate school.

The diagram on page xv illustrates our goals and our progress toward each of these plateaus. In the diagram, note how far down the path the testimony plateau is. Many Latter-day Saints look upon a testimony as the pinnacle of spiritual progress rather than as the beginning of the trail. In the diagram, I have shown testimony as a long plateau just barely out of the world. A testimony that the gospel is true does bring us out of the world, but unless we do something about that testimony, we are barely out, and the world's magnetic pull will tug forcefully on us. If we are not extremely careful, we can find ourselves living in the world and of the world. In Section 1, I discuss how we can strengthen and nourish our testimonies so that we will then move on toward the next plateau.

When we let the principles of the gospel take root in our lives and conduct ourselves in such a way that the Holy Ghost brings about a literal change in us, we begin to progress toward the next plateau, sanctification. In Section 2 we will discuss what sanctification is and how one goes about receiving it. We will learn that it has much to do with receiving the ordinances of the gospel and remaining true to our covenants. We will also review, from a practical standpoint, how the process works. Basically, the way we face our individual trials and tribulations determines to a large degree the velocity at which we travel along this line. Note the distance between the first and second plateaus. It is long and takes most of our time and energy as we sojourn on this earth. It is a process that occurs over a period of time. We could describe the journey as coming unto Christ. Once individuals are sanctified and purified, a mighty change has occurred and they have been born again. This is a literal metamorphosis of the spirit.

The third plateau, spiritual graduate school, is available to those who have become purified to the extent necessary to receive this training. In Section 3 we will talk about mysteries, miracles, and signs and their appropriate roles in our spiritual development. There is a difference between delving into mysteries and having mysteries revealed to us. We will also discuss the reasons for the chronology of the plateaus that I have suggested, and discover that a testimony must be built upon our learning to recognize the still small voice. Without this base, we can be misled by Satan's own miracles, mysteries, and signs. As we take

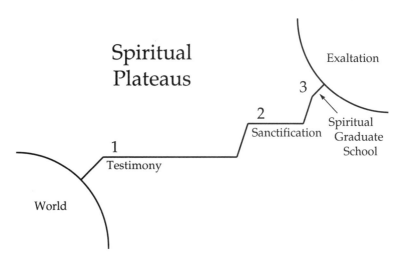

this hike together, I hope to give you a desire to make it to the top as well as the confidence that you can. The Lord loves each of us, and He stands at the top of the trail beckoning us. He also comes to assist and encourage us even when — and perhaps especially when — we may have fallen, sometimes due to our own foolishness. He says to us, as I said to each of our children on their first attempt to climb to the top of Mount Timpanogos, "You can make it. I know it because I know you."

First Plateau

Testimony

1

Gaining a Testimony

The first spiritual plateau of our journey is that of testimony. As in my example of the hike to the top of Mount Timpanogos, a testimony is like the field of flowers that is five miles into the hike. A testimony is beautiful like the flowers. Many Latter-day Saints make it to this point but, because it is so beautiful and comfortable, they cease their effort and never experience the deeper joys of higher plateaus. On the other hand, too many Saints don't even make it this far. They are so busy searching out and hiking every little side trail, often made by sage hens, deer, or rabbits, that they lose their way; and though they may walk a thousand miles, they will never reach the destination of a testimony.

Some members of the Church spend their entire lives exploring every single intellectual side trail rather than staying with the well-marked path. Once atop the first plateau of a testimony, it is easy to look down on all the side trails and see that they lead nowhere. The real path is sometimes narrow, but it is always well marked. Even though the Lord has placed caution signs at forks on the trail, and warned against getting off the trail, many insist on seeing for themselves. Sometimes the result is tragic.

When I use the word *testimony,* I refer to having received a spiritual witness that (1) Jesus is the Christ; (2) Joseph Smith is a prophet of God and was the vehicle through whom the Lord restored the fulness of the gospel and delivered a second witness to Christ known as the Book of Mormon; (3) succeeding prophets received and continue to receive revelation from the Lord relative to our current challenges and the establishment of the kingdom of God on earth; and (4) each of us is entitled to personal revelation in the regulation of our own lives as we live the gospel.

In our most honest moments, many of us question how strong our testimony really is. How does it feel to have the Spirit? Are some of our feelings just wishes, hopes, and desires as opposed to confirmation of the Spirit? How can we be sure? Why can't we testify with the same certainty as others testify?

These questions are particularly troublesome to teenagers and young adults who have grown up in the Church. Converts have a "before" and "after" with which they can compare, but members who have been raised in the Church have not experienced what it is like to be without the Spirit. Many young men and women who are old enough to be called on missions bear their testimonies along this line: "I believe the Church is true, but I'm not really sure. I hope while on my mission I will receive the same testimony many of you have."

Young people often go through their early life leaning on the testimony of parents, grandparents, older brothers and sisters, and the converts who moved in next door. They don't think that anything spectacular has happened to them personally, and so they wait for a feeling of the Spirit that is more powerful than and different from anything they have ever felt before. Then they receive a mission call and realize that they are going to be testifying to people and must be able to stand on their own spiritual feet. They ask themselves, "Do I have a testimony or not?"

Those who pay the price of studying, praying, and living the gospel soon discover a simple truth. They go into the exercise looking for some spectacular spiritual feelings, different from those ever experienced, only to find out they have felt that same familiar spirit all of their life.

The witness a convert receives is the same witness a person born in the Church receives. One reason it is so spectacular to a convert is that it is new. Those who were born in the Church have had these feelings since birth. They have felt them in sacrament meetings, at youth testimony meetings, during family home evenings, while being administered to during an illness, while reading the Book of Mormon, while listening to inspiring stories from their parents, at the airport while seeing brothers or sisters off on missions, while visiting grounds of a temple, when hearing the Joseph Smith story, and so forth. Spiritual witnesses come at a young age to those who are exposed to experiences of a spiritual nature.

I remember vividly something that happened to me at age ten. I grew up in Provo, Utah. Once or twice a year my parents would take my sisters and me to Salt Lake City to visit Temple Square. To entice me to make the pilgrimage, instead of asking if I wanted to go to Temple Square, they would ask, "Do you want to go to the museum where the mummies are?" For readers under forty years of age, I will explain.

In the 1950s there was, on Temple Square, a museum that displayed mummies (among more important things). That was my favorite display. I also enjoyed a display of locks of hair from some of the past prophets, and seeing the watch that President John Taylor was wearing in Carthage Jail when a mob broke in and killed the Prophet Joseph Smith. The watch blocked a bullet that possibly could have taken John Taylor's life — and I could see the bullet hole on that watch. I also enjoyed looking at the death masks of Joseph and his brother Hyrum, who was martyred at the same time as the Prophet. In short, at ten years of age I enjoyed all the gruesome stuff.

On a more positive note, I loved to read the comments that visitors, many of whom were not Latter-day Saints, wrote in the guest register, and I was an enthusiastic collector of all of the free stuff, such as missionary tracts and pamphlets, temple schedules, and calendars, that I could get there. I would go from counter to counter and ask, "Is this free?" When the answer was "Yes," I would take one and carry it with me to the next counter. Sometimes the nice person at the counter would say, "No, I'm sorry, but these cost a nickel." For these occasions, I had perfected a beaten-puppy look of bowing my head and saying, "Oh, I've always wanted to read that pamphlet, but I don't have a nickel." Sigh, sniff, sigh, sniff. More times than not the person would say, "Well, that's all right — I'm sure we won't miss one nickel," and would give me a pamphlet, which I would add to my fistful of free stuff. When I got home, I would proudly and carefully place these things in a neat stack next to the free stuff collected on previous visits.

On this particular occasion we parked across the street from Temple Square at a parking meter in front of what used to be a Walgreen's Drugstore (it is now a bank). At the completion of our tour, my parents made the announcement I had learned to dread: "Glenn, we need to do some shopping. Why don't you stay in the car? We won't be gone long." Then they handed me enough change to feed the parking meter for eight hours.

I tried to busy myself with meaningful activities. I practiced "driving" for a while, until I'm certain the car was flooded. Then I watched the people come out of the drugstore with ice cream cones. Soon I began to keep a tally of how many had bought single cones compared to how many had purchased double cones. When I tired of that, I started keeping track of which flavor was the most popular. Vanilla won. I was appalled.

All of the above may have lasted forty-five minutes, after which I found myself inescapably, critically ill from boredom. Just as I was about to break the cardinal rule of not getting out of the car, I glanced down and saw my stack of free stuff. On the top was a pamphlet that was larger than the others, with a black and white picture of Joseph Smith on the cover and the title "Joseph Smith Tells His Own Story." Ten years later I would distribute copies of that same pamphlet in the mission field.

I was so bored that I decided I might as well read the pamphlet. It was at this point that I had a most memorable experience. I hadn't been reading the pamphlet more than sixty seconds before I became entranced and lost all consciousness of what was going on around me. I became so absorbed that the minutes sped by. When I was approximately halfway through it, something from the outside interrupted my concentration. I looked out the window and then into the rearview mirror. Shocked, I saw that tears were streaming down my cheeks. I couldn't understand what was happening, but I resumed reading and finished the pamphlet without further interruption. However, the tears were still there.

At this point my parents came back and, seeing me in tears, apologized for having been gone so long. They thought I was afraid. As hard as it was for me to let them think my tears resulted from fear, it was easier than to try to explain what had happened. I didn't know what had happened.

It was a long time before I comprehended that I had received an undeniable testimony, at ten years of age, that the Joseph Smith story was true. I didn't hear voices, see angels, or anything like that. What I felt was much stronger. A sixth sense had been touched. I felt elation springing forth from the most inner part of my being, a source protected from the onslaught of deceiving and contriving men—a source that resonates only when touched by the vibration of the Holy Ghost.

Ever since this experience, I have not accepted the enticing, intellectual, ear-tickling debate of the adversary. I have been out-debated on occasions by opponents of the Church, but never converted to their points of view. Even at times when my actions have prevented my feeling the promptings of the Spirit, the memory of how the Spirit feels has kept me from making improper eternal decisions, no matter how enticing they may have appeared. At times when I have felt unworthy to have the Spirit constantly with me, I have thanked and praised God for the memory of those feelings. Because of those memories, I have always known I could never make incorrect decisions that would have permanent, lasting effects. I have always longed to "come home."

I have some friends who might be considered inactive in the Church. Most of them have been born and raised in the Church and exposed to spiritual experiences. Many of them, because of bad habits, don't feel comfortable in formal church settings, but if someone is in need, they are among the first to help. Some of them are occasionally critical of policies and personalities in the Church (which may be their most damaging bad habit), and they will tease me in a good-natured way about my "fanaticism." However, if someone else starts to criticize the Mormons, watch out! They are like a mother grizzly bear defending her cubs. During their life they may have been offended by certain individuals, or they may have transgressed the Lord's commandments and feel unworthy of the Spirit. But deep down they have beautiful feelings about the Church — and, more importantly, they know by the witness of the Spirit that Joseph Smith restored the gospel to the earth and is a prophet of God.

Some time ago I visited with a young woman I had known at a former place of employment. I didn't know she was a Latter-day Saint because I had never heard her mention the Church except in a negative way. On this occasion, after she again criticized the Church, she began asking questions. I answered them as best I could and then added, "It's true, you know. All of it." This seemingly hardened young woman began to cry and said, "I know the Church is true, but I'm not strong enough to do anything about it." Despite her current life-style, the Spirit witnessed again what she had felt at other times. It was unmistakable. I told her what I would say to anyone who may be in a similar circumstance: "Yes you are! The Lord will give you all the strength you need if you will just reach out. Come back. We need you."

A firm testimony is reached when one recognizes the still small voice for what it really is. Once this happens, the commonplace feelings of the Spirit one has experienced throughout his life take upon themselves a very uncommon importance. As we recognize those feelings for what they are, our trust in them increases, and as we exercise faith and live the gospel more precisely, they become stronger. Soon we find that we have developed a sixth sense with which we can test the truth of all things. In addition to sight, smell, touch, hearing, and taste, we can obtain a spiritual feeling that cannot be misled.

Through the sixth sense, we can prove the truth of all things. It will never lie and is never wrong. What does it feel like? It is as difficult to describe as the scent of a rose or the song of a bird or the beauty of a landscape.

The scriptures give us some insights into these feelings. One of the best descriptions of what I felt that day after visiting Temple Square and then reading Joseph Smith's testimony is this passage:

"Verily, verily, I say unto you, I will impart unto you of my Spirit, which shall enlighten your mind, which shall fill your soul with joy; and then shall ye know, or by this shall you know, all things whatsoever you desire of me, which are pertaining unto things of righteousness, in faith believing in me that you shall receive." (D&C 11:13–14.)

As a ten-year-old boy in front of Walgreen's Drugstore, I felt joy. Even though many in our society teach that big boys don't cry, I could not hold back the tears springing forth from a water line that burst when the Spirit connected with the depths of my soul.

In an explanation to Oliver Cowdery about how he could tell when he had found the truth, the Lord said, "If it is right I will cause that your bosom shall burn within you; therefore, you shall feel that it is right." (D&C 9:8.)

Sometimes the feeling is one of peace. The Lord reminded Oliver of this kind of experience: "Verily, verily, I say unto you, if you desire a further witness, cast your mind upon the night that you cried unto me in your heart, that you might know concerning the truth of these things. Did I not speak peace to your mind concerning the matter? What greater witness can you have than from God?" (D&C 6:22–23.)

As inconsistent as it sounds, feeling and hearing the still small voice can shake us to the center. "Yea, thus saith the still small voice, which whispereth through and pierceth all things, and often times it maketh my bones to quake." (D&C 85:6.)

The voice of an angel has had a similar effect. In the Book of Mormon we read about one such experience: "And it came to pass when they heard this voice, and beheld that it was not a voice of thunder, neither was it a voice of a great tumultuous noise, but behold, it was a still voice of perfect mildness, as if it had been a whisper, and it did pierce even to the very soul." (Helaman 5:30.)

A witness of the Spirit sometimes feels like the recalling of a pleasant memory. This is because we knew the gospel once, in our premortal life. President Marion G. Romney once described this form of personal witness: "Man is a dual being. He is composed of a spirit and a body of flesh and bones. His body came into being with his entrance into this world of mortality. His spirit as an individual person was begotten unto God in the spirit world. Through a long period of growth and development, each person's spirit came to know God and spiritual things, including the gospel, obedience to which is a prerequisite to attaining eternal life. Men, however, enter mortality spiritually blind. Never in this life do they recover memory of pre-mortal spiritual things. What they here learn of them must be revealed anew. . . .

"Notwithstanding the fact that during their mortal lives men do not remember anything about their premortal experiences, there still persists in the spirit of every human soul a residuum from his premortal life which instinctively responds to the voice of the Spirit of Christ." (*Look to God and Live,* Salt Lake City: Deseret Book, 1971, pp. 66–67.)

Some truths are revealed gradually over a period of days, weeks, months, or even years. We have to be patient and wait for the witness to come. Alma taught: "Now, we will compare the word unto a seed. Now, if ye give place, that a seed may be planted in your heart, behold, if it be a true seed, or a good seed, if ye do not cast it out by your unbelief, that ye will resist the Spirit of the Lord, behold, it will begin to swell within your breasts; and when you feel these swelling motions, ye will begin to say within yourselves — It must needs be that this is a good seed, or that the word is good, for it beginneth to enlarge my soul; yea, it beginneth to enlighten my understanding, yea, it beginneth to be delicious to me." (Alma 32:28.)

While these scriptures help our understanding, they

fall short because some things can be communicated only spirit to spirit. Although we may not be able to explain the feeling once we have felt it, we cannot deny it. Even as I write these words and review these scriptures, I feel the undeniable witness of the truthfulness of the gospel and am very thankful for it.

You might pause and reflect on what you are feeling right now. I am assuming that you are with me and are feeling that "burning in your bosom." Why? Because what you have read are simple truths, and the Spirit has carried those words into your heart. In spite of the form, the Spirit bears witness of the substance. If you do not feel a witness, or at least do not recognize it for what it is, let me digress long enough to give you some encouragement to keep trying.

The first thing to do is examine your life and see if there is anything out of harmony with the teachings of the Church. Transgression can seriously clog the spiritual lines of communication. If you will make an honest effort to rid yourself of those things, you will be surprised how fast the lines are cleared. Once you have done that, pray to your Father in Heaven fervently that you may know for yourself the truthfulness of the Joseph Smith story and the Book of Mormon, the reality of a living prophet today, and the reality of Jesus Christ, His mission, and the consequence of that mission to you personally.

The question about Joseph Smith is simple. He is either a prophet of God or he is a fraud. It is black or white, with no room for gray. He either saw God the Father and His Son, Jesus Christ, or it is a lie. One might argue that Joseph *thought* he saw a vision and, therefore, he isn't really a perpetrator of falsehood so much as one who has been

misled by either his imaginative mind or the adversary.
But that avoids the issue.

What about the Book of Mormon? It is tangible and it
can be read. Again, there is no room for gray. Joseph Smith
either translated it from ancient tablets or he didn't. It's
as clear as that.

If you doubt the authenticity of Joseph Smith's vision
but believe in a Supreme Being who cares about our welfare
and the truth we are seeking, we have some common
ground. Would God want us to know if He did or did not
speak to Joseph Smith, and if He did or did not have an
angel deliver to Joseph the plates from which the Book of
Mormon was translated? If this is true, He would make it
possible for us to know for ourselves. If it is not true, surely
He would not leave us in the dark, following incorrect
doctrine. Hence, the promise in the Book of Mormon: "And
when ye shall receive these things, I would exhort you
that ye would ask God, the Eternal Father, in the name of
Christ, if these things are not true; and if ye shall ask with
a sincere heart, with real intent, having faith in Christ, he
will manifest the truth of it unto you, by the power of the
Holy Ghost." (Moroni 10:4.)

Those who are honest in heart, if they are willing to
study, pray, and put living the commandments to the test,
have relatively little trouble receiving a witness that Jesus
is the Christ and that Joseph Smith is a prophet of God
and was the vehicle through whom the Lord restored the
gospel in this dispensation. They may also receive a witness that succeeding prophets received and continue to
receive revelation from the Lord. However, it is much
harder for us to have confidence in our own ability to

receive revelation. A partial explanation of this phenomenon is that we are so well aware of our own imperfections.

On April 5, 1985, when I received my call to serve as the second counselor in the Presiding Bishopric, I had not been a regional representative, mission president, stake president, or bishop. I had recently been released as second counselor in our ward bishopric. I knew the Church is true and that we have a living prophet on the earth today, but I didn't know nor could I comprehend why the Lord would call me to this position.

I went to him in prayer and received that same joy I received in my parents' car outside Temple Square thirty-five years earlier relative to the reality of the Joseph Smith story. I knew that the Lord had initiated the call even though I could not comprehend why. This type of personal revelation is available to everyone. It comes as a result of worthiness, not office.

2

Balancing Intellectual with Spiritual Testimony

Once we have received a witness of the Spirit that the Church is true, we need to move on to learning how we can let that same Spirit become a personal guide. It is extremely important that we gain the confidence and faith that we are individually, personally, guided in our lives by that same Spirit which testified to the divinity of Jesus Christ and the truthfulness of the Church. Sometimes our confidence in our ability to receive revelation suffers because we have on occasion misunderstood the Spirit, and we can't figure out what is wrong.

One of the most common mistakes we make is in not paying the intellectual price to justify a confirmation of the Spirit. The opposite is also a problem, because nothing in the gospel can be understood or reasoned out by the intellect alone. How can we avoid relying too much on our intellectual powers while ignoring the Spirit, or expecting spiritual solutions while ignoring our own power to reason things out for ourselves?

Our objective is to reach an elusive balance between two extremes.

On one side of the spectrum are those who tend to trust only in the intellect and thus feel little need to call upon the Lord. Such individuals prefer to be independent and free in their thinking and not tied to the absolute truths of the gospel. They may spend their lives chasing down every intellectual loose end. They take counsel from general or local Church leaders with a grain of salt because, after all, the knowledge of such authorities is minimal when compared to that which so-called scholars have amassed.

The other end of the spectrum may present an even greater threat to the rank-and-file membership of the Church. People on this end of the spectrum think something like this: "I know the Church is true and I have received the gift of the Holy Ghost. I am a worthy member of the Church and, therefore, have access to the Spirit." When faced with a problem they will pray for an answer and then canonize the first thought that comes to mind. I believe that an idea or solution that comes without appropriate reasoning is nothing better than a hunch. There are times of instant inspiration, but they are rare and usually involve an emergency.

Remember what the Lord told Oliver Cowdery when Oliver failed in his attempt to translate the Book of Mormon: "Behold, you have not understood; you have supposed that I would give it unto you, when you took no thought save it was to ask me. But, behold, I say unto you, that you must study it out in your mind; then you must ask me if it be right, and if it is right I will cause that your bosom shall burn within you; therefore, you shall feel that it is right. But if it be not right you shall have no such feelings, but you shall have a stupor of thought." (D&C 9:7–9.)

Of this scripture Elder Bruce R. McConkie commented: "Implicit in asking in faith is the precedent requirement that we do everything in our power to accomplish the goal that we seek. We use the agency with which we have been endowed. We use every faculty and capacity and ability that we possess to bring about the eventuality that may be involved. . . . There's a fine balance between agency and inspiration." (*Speeches of the Year: BYU Devotional Addresses, 1972–1973,* pp. 110, 113.)

President Romney put it this way: "When confronted with a problem I prayerfully weigh in my mind alternative solutions and come to a conclusion as to which of them is best. Then in prayer I submit to the Lord my problem, tell him I desire to make the right choice, what is, in my judgment, the right course. Then I ask him if I have made the right decision to give me the burning in my bosom that He promised Oliver Cowdery. . . . When we learn to distinguish between the inspiration that comes from the Spirit of the Lord and that which comes from our own uninspired hopes and desires, we need make no mistakes." (*New Era,* October 1975, p. 35.)

This doctrine is so simple and straightforward that we might feel guilty admitting we have difficulty with its application. How do we determine when we have done enough homework and, consequently, we have a right to a spiritual confirmation? How can we become masters at knowing when we have received a spiritual witness?

There is a sentence used in church circles that sends a chill up my spine. It is a perfectly good sentence and packs a spiritual wallop when used by someone who has been acted upon by the Spirit, but unfortunately it is used too often by those who have wandered off center in the spectrum. The sentence is this: "I feel real good about it." Every time I hear it, I see a red flag go up. It is a perfectly good way of expressing a feeling of the Spirit, but too often the literal translation is, "I haven't done my homework." Some bad decisions have been made by people who "feel really good" about something they have failed to reason out in their minds.

Several years ago I learned a great lesson while laboring as the managing director of the Church's Welfare Services Department. We were at a critical stage in the history of Church welfare, and it was time to go through an agonizing reappraisal of the program in light of current world conditions.

After praying for a solution to the problems we faced, I had a terrific thought: *Glenn, you have access to the Quorum of the Twelve and to a member of the First Presidency.* What a resource! I called for appointments and met individually with these great men. I poured out my concerns and added my feeling that we were at a stage where further revelation on the subject was necessary. Then I sat back with my pen and yellow notepad and waited for pearls of wisdom. I was devastated when their collective counsel amounted to this: "Brother Pace, we commend you for your concern and conscientiousness in finding solutions to these weighty matters. We, too, have some deep concerns and anxieties, and you are absolutely right—we do need revelation. Now, go get it!"

Who, me? I was an employee of the Church, not a General Authority. However, I had been taught that I had the responsibility to take to the Brethren well-thought-out recommendations that could be confirmed, modified, or rejected in the appropriate forums. It was my obligation and right to receive inspiration. And I knew that inspiration would come only after intense, agonizing study, research, and meditation. In other words, I learned that revelation is 95 percent hard work.

We can learn from President Spencer W. Kimball's experience in receiving the revelation on the priesthood. He used both intellectual and spiritual faculties prior to receiving that revelation. He explained the process:

"As you know, on the ninth of June a policy was changed that affects great numbers of people throughout the world. Millions and millions of people will be affected by the revelation which came. I remember very vividly that day after day I walked to the temple and ascended to the fourth floor where we have our solemn assemblies and where we have our meetings of the Twelve and the First Presidency. After everybody had gone out of the temple, I knelt and prayed. I prayed with much fervency. I knew that something was before us that was extremely important to many of the children of God. I knew that we could receive the revelations of the Lord only by being worthy and ready for them and ready to accept them and put them into place. Day after day I went alone and with great solemnity and seriousness in the upper rooms of the temple, and there I offered my soul and my efforts to go forward with the program. I wanted to do what he wanted. I talked about it to him and told him, 'Lord, I want only what is right. We are not making any plans to be spectacularly moving. We want only the thing that thou dost want, and we want it when you want it and not until.'

"We met with the Council of the Twelve Apostles, time after time, in the holy room where there is a picture of the Savior in many different moods and also pictures of all the Presidents of the Church. Finally we had the feeling and the impression from the Lord, who made it very clear to us, that this was the thing to do to make the gospel universal to all worthy people." (*Teachings of Spencer W. Kimball,* Salt Lake City: Bookcraft, 1982, pp. 450–51.)

President Kimball had to use every intellectual faculty at his disposal prior to receiving a spiritual witness.

In receiving personal revelation, we must not depend entirely on our own intellect. We can learn much from the problems the Church went through concerning some false historical documents a few years ago. The lessons on straying off center are vivid. To those who may lean toward this end of the spectrum, I would ask a soul-searching question: "Would the discovery of any document, no matter how contradictory to what you believe to be true, shake your testimony?" The discovery might raise some intellectual questions, but if it shakes a person's testimony, I would submit that that person really doesn't have one. Those who rely entirely on intellect may point at those whose testimony cannot and will not be shaken and accuse them of blind faith. The very fact that they would make such an accusation suggests they have not yet learned there is an avenue to truth greater than intellect and more certain than the five senses. They have left unexplored the most glorious of all avenues to truth—direct revelation from heaven.

On this subject, George Q. Cannon said: "We are asked whether it is possible for a man, by means of his five senses alone independent of the Holy Ghost, to know that Joseph Smith is a Prophet of the living God. . . .

"To begin with the perfect use of our senses is only given to us by the aid of the Spirit of God and the light that cometh from Him; and while it is possible for men to reason upon various subjects and satisfy their minds concerning truth, still the highest testimony that a human being can have respecting Joseph Smith being a Prophet or of our Lord Jesus being the Savior is the testimony of the Holy Ghost. The Lord has given light and intelligence to His children by means of which they are able to arrive at a knowledge concerning many things. This is done through the instrumentality of the Spirit of God. Men can satisfy themselves that Jesus is the Savior of the world by reasoning upon it and adducing evidences that are open to the outer senses, and yet they cannot reach such a conclusion without the aid of the Spirit of God. Paul says: 'No man can say that Jesus is the Lord, but by the Holy Ghost.' (1 Corinthians 12:3.) The same may be said in relation to the knowledge of Joseph Smith being a Prophet of God.

"For a man to say he knows a spiritual truth by the aid of his outer senses, is a rash and ill-considered expression, and it should not give rise to discussion." (*Gospel Truth,* Deseret Book, 1987, pp. 270–71.)

Does all this mean we should not pursue knowledge with our five senses? Should we not study history? I love Church history. I am thankful we know the location of the

Sacred Grove, the Hill Cumorah, the site for the temple in Jackson County, Nauvoo, Adam-ondi-Ahman, Liberty Jail, and other Church sites. My joy when visiting these areas is intensified by knowing what took place there. However, the most lasting impressions obtained by these visits is what is felt there rather than what is remembered.

On one occasion, my wife and I visited some of these sites. Two experiences come to mind that are relevant to this search for balance. In Jackson County we sat on the lawn at sunset within the boundaries of the future Jackson County temple. We talked of history and of prophecies of the future. But what we remember most vividly is the sweet, peaceful, spiritual witness that Jesus Christ stands at the head of His church today and that Joseph Smith is what he claimed to be, a prophet of God.

No amount of historical research alone could bring to pass that spiritual witness. It comes only when we become attuned and learn to recognize spiritual things. However, the spiritual witness was intensified by our knowledge of what has happened there in Jackson County and what will yet happen there. That evening we found the elusive balance.

The next day we strayed off center. We went to Adam-ondi-Ahman, part of a sacred past and destined to be included in a sacred future. Knowing this history helped us understand the significance of the land. We had a history book that told of an altar of Adam and of the Nephites and that even gave the exact location. We did not know at the time that subsequent research has given rise to some questions on the exact location of the altar. We arrived one hour before sunset, and in our search of the precise location as described in that book, we drove to and fro, becoming more frustrated by the minute. We climbed over fences, walked through fields, stampeded cattle, and soon found ourselves in a very vile mood.

Fortunately, we came to our senses and drove to a knoll just in time to watch the sunset and enjoy the spirit of the place. Again, the Lord blessed us with a spiritual experience we can recall vividly.

Often we see people becoming so involved in the search for historical and archeological details that they fail to take advantage of spiritual experiences right before their eyes. The same historical knowledge that can intensify spiritual experiences can destroy spirituality when one strays too far off center. A complete testimony was never intended to be gained through history or other scholarly source except that which has been kept by prophets and that which comes forth as scripture. A saving testimony will never come from a spectacular historical or archeological find.

If the Lord meant for our testimonies to be based on physical, historical evidence rather than scripture—if we needed to have such evidence to validate our testimonies, rather than relying on faith and inspiration—He could certainly give us such evidence. To illustrate, while I was on my mission, the question I dreaded most was "Where are the golden plates today?" I did not enjoy the looks my companion and I got when we answered, "The angel took them back." I didn't comprehend then what I know now. If we had been able to take Moroni and the plates from door to door, the number of converts would not have increased. Without a confirmation of the Spirit, they would not have believed or would have found some way to explain away what they were seeing.

Remember what the Lord told Joseph Smith regarding

Martin Harris's desire to see the plates: "Behold, if they will not believe my words, they would not believe you, my servant Joseph, if it were possible that you should show them all these things which I have committed unto you." (D&C 5:7.)

The only way to gain a testimony is through the way given in the promise of Moroni. Spiritual manifestations are generally reserved for those who are spiritually mature, not just as a reward for faith, but also to assure that sacred things are not mocked. A person must become adept at recognizing the Spirit before a spiritual manifestation can be a sanctifying experience. Numerous examples in the scriptures show how pointless a physical manifestation can be without the accompanying receipt of the witness of the Holy Ghost. Conversion does not come by physical manifestations from heaven.

Laman and Lemuel observed many miraculous manifestations such as this one recorded by their brother Nephi: "After the angel had spoken unto us, he departed. And after the angel had departed, Laman and Lemuel again began to murmur, saying: How is it possible that the Lord will deliver Laban into our hands? Behold, he is a mighty man, and he can command fifty, yea, even he can slay fifty; then why not us?" Nephi couldn't believe what his brothers were saying. He responded, "Ye also know that an angel hath spoken unto you; wherefore can ye doubt?" (1 Nephi 3:30–31; 4:3.) Here we have an example of knowledge being of no eternal value because the Spirit was absent.

Nephi later put his finger on Laman and Lemuel's problem: "Ye are swift to do iniquity but slow to remember the Lord your God. Ye have seen an angel, and he spake unto you; yea, ye have heard his voice from time to time; and he hath spoken unto you in a still small voice, but ye were past feeling." (1 Nephi 17:45.)

Even in heavenly manifestations we must acquire the ability to recognize the Spirit and feel as well as see and hear the experience. Were it not so, Satan could thoroughly confuse us with his own demonstrations. Despite all the spectacular manifestations received by the Nephites and Lamanites at the birth of the Savior, within a short time doubts crept into the minds of those who were not converted. "The people began to forget those signs and wonders which they had heard, and began to be less and less astonished at a sign or a wonder from heaven, insomuch that they began to be hard in their hearts, and blind in their minds, and began to disbelieve all which they had heard and seen—imagining up some vain thing in their hearts, that it was wrought by men and by the power of the devil, to lead away and deceive the hearts of the people." (3 Nephi 2:1–2.)

If a witness of the Spirit is necessary to discern the validity of a visit by an angel, how very vital that witness is in more subtle situations.

While we should constantly improve our scholarship on every wholesome subject, it is not necessary to reserve judgment on the reality of the complete gospel until all the evidence is in. To do so would be to stumble through life with so much uncertainty that the gospel could not begin to have a personal effect on us, and the whole plan of the gospel would be frustrated as far as our personal life is concerned. We must accept the premise that when all of the data are in, every gospel principle will be proven scientifically sound.

We all bump into some intellectual stumbling blocks. We see some of them disappear as we gain spiritual and intellectual maturity, while others seem to remain with us. However, once we have received that witness, to refuse to accept the gospel as being true because we do not have answers to all of our intellectual questions would be like refusing to believe that the Savior raised Lazarus from the dead because we cannot figure out what scientific process took place to restore life.

3

Inappropriate
Intellectualism

Should we have questions? Of course. However, some people seem to relish in turning every answer into a question. Elder John A. Widtsoe said:

"Doubt, which ever is or should be a passing condition, must never itself be an end. Doubt as an objective of life is an intellectual and a spiritual offense. A lasting doubt implies an unwillingness on the part of the individual to seek the solution of his problem, or a fear to face the truth. Doubt should vanish as it appears, or as soon as proper inquiry can place it either with the known or the unknown facts of life; with the solvable or the unsolvable; with the knowable or the unknowable.

"The strong man is not afraid to say, 'I do not know'; the weak man simpers and answers, 'I doubt.' Doubt, unless transmuted into inquiry, has no value or worth in the world. Of itself it has never lifted a brick, driven a nail, or turned a furrow. To take pride in being a doubter, without earnestly seeking to remove the doubt, is to reveal shallowness of thought and purpose. . . .

"Doubt of the right kind — that is, honest questioning — leads to faith. Such doubt impels men to inquiry which always opens the door to truth. . . .

"Joseph Smith is an excellent example of proper doubt. The ministers of his day were contending for the membership of the boy. He went to God for help; received it; and doubt disappeared. From that day on, doubt did not reappear. His doubt was lost in the desired knowledge he gained from proper inquiry. So may every man do.

"The unknown universe, material, mental, spiritual, is greater than the known. If we seek, we shall forever add knowledge to knowledge. That which seems dark today, will be crystal clear tomorrow. Eternal progress means the unending elucidation of things not known or understood today.

"No! Doubt is not wrong unless it becomes an end of life. It rises to high dignity when it becomes an active search for, and practice of, truth. Doubt which immediately leads to honest inquiry, and thereby removes itself, is wholesome. But that doubt which feeds and grows upon itself, and, with stubborn indolence, breeds more doubt, is evil." (*Evidences and Reconciliations*, Salt Lake City: Bookcraft, 1987, pp. 31–33.)

I am saddened from time to time to learn that certain of my friends are wasting their lives nailing down every intellectual loose end. They nail down one tentacle and another one always pops up. My favorite statement on this subject is from Richard Hofstadter: "Ideally, the pursuit of truth is said to be at the heart of the intellectual's business. . . . As with the pursuit of happiness, the pursuit of truth is itself gratifying. . . . Truth captured loses its glamor; . . . easy truths are a bore. . . . Whatever the intellectual is too certain of, if he is healthily playful, he begins to find unsatisfactory. The meaning of his intellectual life lies not in the possession of truth but in the quest for new uncertainties. Harold Rosenberg . . . said that the intellectual is one who turns answers into questions." (*Anti-intellectualism in American Life*, New York: Alfred A. Knopf, 1963, p. 30.)

Dr. Hugh Nibley, noted scholar and writer at Brigham Young University, has written: "The scholar . . . must necessarily get [his] knowledge from the written word. . . . The prophet . . . who may well be illiterate, gets his knowledge by direct intercourse with heaven. The orientation of the two is entirely different. . . . The prophet recognizes the scholar for what he is, but the scholar does not return the compliment. He cannot conceive how anyone could possibly acquire knowledge by any method other than his. He cannot believe that any man has experienced anything which he has not experienced." (*The World and the Prophets*, vol. 3, The Collected Works of Hugh Nibley, Salt Lake City: Deseret Book, 1987, pp. 28, 31.)

Elder James E. Faust has expressed this idea in a quaint way: "An intellectual is a person who chases after a bus even after he has caught up with it."

Intellectual conversion is not lasting. Being touched by the Spirit is. While on my mission in the Boston, Massachusetts, area, I thrived on meeting with students. I enjoyed debating with intellectuals on points of doctrine and philosophy. On one occasion a new companion and I were meeting with a young married couple. My companion, a "greenie," was petrified because the couple were asking questions that weren't in the discussions. They would ask him a question and as he turned pale, I would jump in and rescue him by saying something profound or, if I couldn't think of profundity, at least something clever. After all, I had been in the mission field for over a year.

Finally the husband turned to me, very irritated, and said, "Elder Pace, with all due respect, we would like to hear what your companion has to say." My companion, in effect, bore his sweet, simple testimony. When he concluded, the couple were speechless and tears filled their eyes. I knew he had taught them more in his one-minute testimony than I had taught them in ten hours of previous debate.

After being in the mission field a while, missionaries can become adept at discerning those who feel the Spirit, those who invite them back because they think the missionaries are nice individuals, and those who simply enjoy intellectual gymnastics. Missionaries also experience the joy of looking someone in the eye as they bear witness, and can know that the person recognizes the message. It is as if the person has been reminded of a forgotten, pleasant experience, as the veil of forgetfulness has been pierced. Some will cry. Some will send the missionaries away because they are afraid to know more. Others will invite the missionaries back so they can feast more upon the word. And some have the courage of their convictions and are baptized.

On some occasions, the Spirit will provide assurance that a witness has been given and felt by an investigator even as he or she is asking some tough questions and is being antagonistic. I have interrupted people at times and said, "Let's talk about that later. Right now I want to talk about what you are feeling. You're feeling like we're reminding you of beautiful things you had forgotten. You're feeling that we are telling you the truth. You're feeling like you've come home after a long absence. You're feeling peace. You're feeling the Holy Ghost. You will feel it when we teach. You will feel it when you read the Book of Mormon. Learn to recognize it and rely on it. It will lead you to the truth." I have seen people sob as they first recognize the beautiful witness of the Comforter.

I returned to the mission field ten years after my mission and looked up a convert who had subsequently left the Church. We talked for many hours. She explained how she was now participating in another church where she was free to engage in lively discussion on her personal views of eternal things. "There is no right and wrong in that church," she told me. "The people there are truly loving and tolerant. They are all searching for truth rather than trying to impose their views on others, and I really feel free."

I reminded her, after listening to her story, "Ten years ago you were baptized. Do you remember the feelings you had then and that you recognized in other new converts? You called it 'the glow.' You felt it. It was different from anything you had felt before. Remember? All this intellectual mumbo-jumbo you've been giving me for the last two hours is worthless compared to that feeling. How could you forget it?"

She bowed her head and looked at the floor, then up into my eyes, and said, "I haven't." At that moment I received a witness that she was feeling it again, so I said,

"Furthermore, you're feeling it again right now, aren't you?" She cried and then asked, "Why did you have to come back?" I replied, "Because the Lord loves you."

Several years went by, and then she came to Salt Lake City. Since our last visit, tragedy had come into her life. I thought perhaps the time had finally come when she would give up her intellectualism and follow the promptings of the Spirit, but my hopes were shattered after the pleasantries had been taken care of.

She said, "I know it's hard for you to take, but I'm very happy with my current beliefs and friends. They are stimulating to be with and have been very supportive." She said this in a tone that meant, "There really are some good people outside the Mormon church, in case you hadn't noticed."

I said, "All right, we've established one can be intelligent and kind without being a Mormon. Now what would you like to talk about?" Three hours later, we had rehashed all the questions she had ever had about the Church. At the conclusion I said, "Oh my, *déja vu*. Here we go again. Twenty-five years later at the same impasse." As usual, I was drained and frustrated.

While she was in Salt Lake City, my wife and I took her to Temple Square. I'll never forget walking up the circular ramp leading to the statue of the Christus in the visitor's center. Halfway up the ramp, she paused and said, "Oh dear, here comes that feeling again." Tears filled her eyes, and absolutely nothing was said for the next thirty minutes as we sat in front of the statue. Tears flowed freely down her cheeks. The following Sunday my wife took her to the Tabernacle Choir broadcast and the scene was repeated. No words were needed as the Spirit flowed into her spiritual memory bank and brought back sweet, comforting truths.

The last words spoken before she returned to Boston went something like this: "Yes, I felt that feeling again that I only feel around Mormons," she told me, "but I just can't seem to let go of my way of life. Does that mean I am a bad person? What would be my judgment should I die tomorrow?" My response to the first question was "No," and to the second, "I don't know. All I know is that the Lord continues to allow you to feel His spirit, which means He hasn't given up on you or written you off. How long He will leave the door open is known only to Him."

Some people may not join the Church. Some may join and then leave, but once they have felt the Spirit, they can never dismiss it as something trivial. This is conversion — spirit touching spirit.

How, then, do we keep our spiritual perspective relative to the elusive balance between intellectually doing our homework and relying on a power beyond our own intellect? The ability to discern spiritual promptings is one that is developed. We learn by doing it. Have you ever been certain you have received a spiritual witness, only to have subsequent events prove you were in error? Have you ever had a spiritual witness you ignored because it seemed illogical, only to find out you should have listened?

We have more patience with our failures in learning to ski than we do in learning to recognize the Spirit. When we fall going down the slope, we get up, laugh at ourselves, and try again. But when we have a failure in recognizing the Spirit, we feel guilty and are reluctant to go forward. It's natural to have spiritual setbacks. The important thing is that we don't give up.

We all know that it takes years of practice to become a professional athlete, and that a price must be paid. How, then, can we expect to be an overnight success in spiritual things? Joseph Smith said this: "A person may profit by noticing the first intimation of the spirit of revelation; for instance, when you feel pure intelligence flowing into you, it may give you sudden strokes of ideas, so that by noticing it, you may find it fulfilled the same day or soon; (i.e.) those things that were presented unto your minds by the Spirit of God, will come to pass; and thus by learning the Spirit of God and understanding it, *you may grow into the principle of revelation,* until you become perfect in Christ Jesus." (*Teachings of the Prophet Joseph Smith,* Salt Lake City: Deseret Book, 1976, p. 151. Italics added.)

Elder Widtsoe explained: "It is a paradox that men will gladly devote time every day for many years to learn a science or an art; yet will expect to win a knowledge of the gospel, which comprehends all sciences and arts, through perfunctory glances at books or occasional listening to sermons. The gospel should be studied more intensively than any school or college subject. They who pass opinion on the gospel without having given it intimate and careful study are not lovers of truth, and their opinions are worthless." (*Evidences and Reconciliations,* pp. 16–17.)

To become proficient in basketball, players have to practice shooting countless shots. By repeating successful approaches and changing failures, they finally get the uncanny ability of knowing, as soon as the ball leaves their hands, whether or not the shot will be good. In spiritual things we need to learn to recognize when we have had a witness of the Spirit, and we must be able to recognize a counterfeit thrown at us by Satan or self-imposed by our own ambition and desire.

Sometimes a young man will tell his girlfriend, "I have received a spiritual witness that you are to be my wife." In some cases the witness may be more a desire than a manifestation. If a young man receives such a witness, he should put it to the test and ask her to marry him. If she says yes, he was right. If she says no, he was wrong. In any event, the young woman is perfectly capable of receiving her own revelation on the matter.

If it were possible, I would lay down a formula for instant and certain success. But one of the reasons it is so hard to enjoy consistent success is that the variables change each day. We are often more in tune with the Spirit on one day than on another. We may be more vulnerable emotionally on one day than on another. Satan may work harder on us on one day than another. However, with all the variables there is one constant: The Spirit witnesses only to the truth.

If your success ratio for recognizing the Spirit is low, ask yourself these questions:

1. How well am I living the commandments?

2. Am I studying the scriptures in order to be more attuned to spiritual things?

3. Am I praying with real intent?

4. Have I done my homework and gone to the Lord with a well-thought-out solution?

5. Have I learned to recognize a stupor of thought?

6. Can I honestly say "Thy will be done," and am I willing to take no for an answer?

We have to learn to recognize the Spirit in personal revelations and to close in on that elusive balance between intellectual solutions and the promptings of the Spirit. While it is not always easy to obtain personal revelation to guide one's own life, obtaining a testimony of the truthfulness of the gospel is relatively easy. Unfortunately, many make it difficult because they insist on giving every single precept an intellectual shakedown prior to accepting it.

4

Criticism
and Critics

Nothing squelches the Spirit more than for an individual, after once having received a witness of the truthfulness of the gospel, to allow questions to turn into doubts, doubts into frustration, and frustration into criticism of the Lord's anointed. Sometimes criticism comes as a result of members feeling they must justify our beliefs to the pointing fingers and mocking voices coming from "the great and spacious building" that Lehi saw in vision:

"After they had partaken of the fruit of the tree they did cast their eyes about as if they were ashamed. And I also cast my eyes round about, and beheld, on the other side of the river of water, a great and spacious building; and it stood as it were in the air, high above the earth. And it was filled with people, both old and young, both male and female; and their manner of dress was exceedingly fine; and they were in the attitude of mocking and pointing their fingers towards those who had come at and were partaking of the fruit. And after they had tasted of the fruit they were ashamed, because of those that were scoffing at them; and they fell away into forbidden paths and were lost." (1 Nephi 8:25–28.)

To a certain degree, we are all somewhat susceptible to pressures around us.

One day when one of my sons bade me farewell as he left for high school, I noticed he had forgotten to tie his shoelaces. For a fleeting second I was tempted to turn the moment into the major crisis of the week, but, thankfully, I let it pass.

A few days later at a school function I observed, to my amazement, that the shoelaces of all of the young men were untied. I then realized my son had fallen victim to another fad. I think it was in this same year that I found out it was no longer socially acceptable to go to school with boots, gloves, or ear muffs.

Sometimes we appear to be enslaved by fads and trends in society. Some are good. Some are silly but harmless. Others can be detrimental to our physical or spiritual health. It never ceases to amaze me how some members of the Church are so sensitive to pressure from a world that has no spiritual perspective whatsoever.

Knowing that the shortest distance from the world to the celestial kingdom is a straight line, the Lord has restored His gospel, which contains the truth and guidance we need in order to make the journey as smooth as possible. We can avoid unnecessary detours by reading the scriptures and listening to the Lord's anointed prophets. As the Church holds firm to the traditional values taught by prophets of previous dispensations and reaffirmed by our modern-day prophets, the pointing finger of a failing society seems to be regularly aimed at us. One can hardly get through a day without hearing some form of criticism about the Church. The criticism comes from three groups: nonmembers, former members, and current members.

Teasing and criticism from nonmembers are often harmless. In fact, such comments can help keep us on our toes. Occasionally we need to step back and look at ourselves from a nonmember's perspective. Really, to them don't we sometimes appear to be just a little bit strange? Imagine yourself coming into a Mormon community for the first time and hearing talk about gold plates, an angel named Moroni, and baptisms for the dead. Imagine seeing, for the first time, nine children and two beleaguered parents in a beat-up station wagon with a bumper sticker reading "Families are forever." The puzzled nonmember doesn't know if this is a boast or a complaint. And where do these families go to church? A stake house. We may truly seem strange to nonmembers—until they get to know us.

In this regard, my counsel to members would be to relax, lighten up, mellow out, and not get so huffy. While the gospel is sacred and serious, sometimes we take ourselves a little too seriously. A sense of humor, especially about ourselves, is an attribute worthy of development. But we should not allow the teasing and questions to derail us from the knowledge we have received from the witness of the Spirit, and to sidetrack us into endless, meaningless debate.

Some criticisms of nonmembers may be a little more painful—criticism always hurts most when we deserve it.

For example, it may be aimed at active Latter-day Saints who don't live up to what they have been taught and who may be condescending, intolerant, or clannish. Such characteristics strike at the very heart of the second great commandment, "Thou shalt love thy neighbour as thyself." (Matthew 22:39.) One can be a friend to all without participating in all of their activities. How shortsighted we are if we place denominational limits on our friendships. How sad it is if we rob ourselves by making our friendship contingent upon another's willingness to listen to the first missionary discussion. We would eliminate the most painful criticism from responsible nonmembers by simply internalizing our testimonies and living what the Spirit has witnessed to us.

The second category of critics is comprised of former members who have become disenchanted with the Church but who are obsessed with making vicious and vile attacks upon it. Most members and nonmembers alike see such attacks for what they really are. What credibility can possibly be given to a person who mocks beliefs held sacred by another? Anyone who would resort to such attacks unwittingly discloses his or her true character; or lack of the same. As Latter-day Saints, we are appalled by such attacks. We would hope that they would make us more sensitive to the sacred beliefs of others and careful not to make light of those beliefs. We should waste no time in defending ourselves from those who have chosen to listen to a voice of the adversary.

In addition to attacking our sacred beliefs, some former members speak evil of the Brethren. Joseph Smith received his share of this kind of criticism from the dissidents of his day. The Lord's revelation to him is applicable to us today: "Cursed are all those that shall lift up the heel against mine anointed, saith the Lord, and cry they have sinned when they have not sinned before me, saith the Lord, but have done that which was meet in mine eyes, and which I commanded them. But those who cry transgression do it because they are the servants of sin, and are the children of disobedience themselves." (D&C 121:16–17.)

It seems that history continues to teach us: You can leave the Church, but you can't leave it alone. The basic reason for this is simple. Once someone has received a witness of the Spirit and accepted it, that person leaves neutral ground. People can lose their testimonies only by listening to the promptings of the evil one, and Satan's goal is not complete when such individuals leave the Church, but only when they come out in open rebellion against it.

The third source of criticism is within the Church itself. This kind of criticism is more lethal than that which comes from nonmembers and former members. The danger lies not in what might come from members who are critical, but in the chance that we might join them with our own criticisms. Nothing will destroy a testimony faster than for a person to openly rebel or criticize the Lord's anointed.

Member critics testify that they know the *gospel* is true but they believe the *Brethren* are just a little out of touch. Out of touch with what? Don't confuse a decision to abstain from participating in a trend in society with a lack of awareness about its existence. These Brethren "prove all things" and "hold fast that which is good." (1 Thessalonians 5:21.) To accomplish this, they are in constant touch with Him who created this earth and knows the world from beginning to end.

I am amazed at the egotism of those members who suggest that without debate on certain issues, the prophet would not know what questions to ask the Lord. Regarding those who feel inclined to steady the ark, President Joseph F. Smith said: "It is very unfortunate for a man to be taken in this snare; for be it understood by the Latter-day Saints that as long as the servants of God are living pure lives, are honoring the Priesthood conferred upon them, and endeavoring to the best of their knowledge to magnify their offices and callings, to which they have been duly chosen by the voice of the people and the priesthood, and sanctioned by the approval of God, so long as the Lord has any communication to make to the children of men, or any instructions to impart to his Church, he will make such communication through the legally appointed channel of the priesthood; he will never go outside of it, as long, at least, as the Church of Jesus Christ of Latter-day Saints exists in its present form on the earth." (*Gospel Doctrine*, Salt Lake City: Deseret Book, 1986, p. 41.)

On the same subject, Elder John A. Widtsoe said: "There are many attacks by the evil one upon a weakening testimony. Commonly, a feeling of superiority, ending in ambition for office, overshadows all else and leads to testimony starvation. Personal ambition has always been a destructive force in human lives. Sometimes, and closely related to the feeling of superiority, [there] are false interpretations of scripture. These rise to such magnitude, though at variance with accepted, revealed doctrine, that they endanger the spiritual life of the individual. The various cults that arise, like mushrooms, from time to time, are but variations of this manner of destroying a testimony. They can always be recognized, for they are in opposition to some principle or regulation of the Church.

"Most frequently, however, the loss of a testimony is due to finding fault with one's fellow believers, and with the leadership of the Church. Every action of bishop, stake president, or General Authority seems wrong, to such unfortunate people. Their vision distorts the world and all in it." (*Evidences and Reconciliations,* p. 40.)

Some Latter-day Saints practice selective obedience. A prophet is not one who displays a smorgasbord of truth from which we are free to pick and choose. However, some persons become critical and suggest that the prophet should change the menu. A prophet doesn't take a poll to see which way the wind of public opinion is blowing. He reveals the will of the Lord to us. The world is full of deteriorating churches whose leaders have succumbed to public opinion and have become more dedicated to tickling the ears of their members than obeying the laws of God.

In the early days of the Restoration, some converts wanted to bring a few of their previous beliefs into the Church with them. Our problem today is with members who seem vulnerable to the trends in society (and the pointing fingers that attend them) and want the Church to change its position to accommodate them. The doctrinal grass on the other side of the fence looks very green to them.

The Lord's counsel in 1831 is relevant today: "Behold, I say unto you, that they desire to know the truth in part, but not all, for they are not right before me and must needs repent." (D&C 49:2.) We need to accept the full truth, "put on the whole armour of God" (Ephesians 6:11), and get to work building up the kingdom.

5

Making Our
Commitment

A time must come in our lives when we make a basic decision. Is the gospel true? Yes! Then let's get on with what is expected of us. We might also ask ourselves, Do I contribute in a positive way toward the building up of the kingdom?

A testimony is serious business. Once we have it, we need to do something about it. I would remind you that the first plateau is only the beginning. It is kindergarten. We need to get on to graduate school. Too many of us view the obtaining and retaining of a testimony as our ultimate goal. If we find that our testimony is fading, we tend to immerse ourselves in studying, praying, and serving until we once again feel that familiar spirit, and then we rejoice in the fact that our testimony has come back. At that point, rather than lying down in the flowers of the first plateau and taking a nap, we should resolve to do more and prepare to move on to the next plateau.

In the mission field, my companion and I were teaching a Harvard University student. After we told him the Joseph Smith story and bore our testimonies to him, as we had done many times before, he said, "Wait a minute. Are you telling me you believe God and Christ appeared to Joseph Smith and told him he was to set up a new church?" We said we did believe that. He continued the interrogation: "You also believe an angel gave plates to Joseph Smith, who translated them into the Book of Mormon, and that the Savior appeared to the people on this continent?" We said we did. "You also believe the president of your church is a prophet who receives revelation from God, as did Adam, Noah, and Abraham?" We said we did. Getting more animated by the minute, the investigator said, "That is the most incredible story I have ever heard. If I really believed all of that, I wouldn't be able to sleep. I would run down the streets screaming it to everyone. Why aren't you more excited about it?" That was a penetrating question.

Do you have a testimony? What are you doing about it? As the Harvard student implied, a testimony is not enough. A testimony that Joseph Smith saw God and the Savior is meaningless unless that fact begins to mean something to each of us individually.

A few years ago I was going through a much needed spiritual renaissance. As part of that rejuvenation I read two sets of books on the history of the Church: *A Comprehensive History of the Church,* by B. H. Roberts, and *History of the Church,* by Joseph Smith. These sets consist of a total of thirteen volumes, and it took me approximately two years to read them. In the course of my reading, I found myself absolutely captivated by Joseph Smith — emotionally, intellectually, and spiritually. As I read the revelations he received and the letters written by him and to him and about him, I gained a great testimony of the divinity of his mission here upon the earth.

I once again received an undeniable testimony, just as I had at ten years of age. However, at age thirty-five I was better able to appreciate what the Prophet accomplished in his thirty-eight years. I caught myself wishing I had been born during his ministry. As I read about the dissenters and traitors, I wondered why I could not have been born then instead of now. After all, he needed all of the help he could get, and I would not have betrayed him. If I had been born then, I would have done everything in my power to help him with the work. But then I asked myself: Are you sure? Are you sure you would have been valiant? You would have given your life for Joseph Smith, but what are you doing for the prophet and president of the Church today? You would die for Joseph Smith, but you are not willing to accept a home teaching assignment to visit more than two families.

Why do we sometimes find it easier to accept and follow past prophets? It is partly because history has proven their counsel to be sound. Future generations will find the same to be true of the prophets of our day. Each of us might ask ourselves, What am I doing for our current, living prophet?

As I finished reading those histories of the Church, I came to a realization, as powerful as my testimony of Joseph Smith, on this issue. I was allowed to see into my own soul deeply enough to recognize the following: If, by some miracle, the Lord changed my place in time and I found myself living in Nauvoo at the time Joseph was there, how valiant would I have been? A witness of the Spirit gave me an answer I didn't like, but I knew it was true at that point in my life. I received the conviction that with my current spiritual quotient, I would not have been valiant had I been with Joseph. This was a devastating revelation to me.

This experience taught me firsthand that a testimony is not enough. I had just finished thirteen volumes about the life of Joseph Smith and I knew he was a prophet, but I wasn't doing much about it. Therefore, I realized, the gospel was not changing my life. I decided right then that I was going to be more submissive to what the Lord would have me do now, in this period of time, inasmuch as this is when He chose to have me come to the earth. In effect, I laid everything on the altar. The gospel is true. What would the Lord have me do about it?

Since being called to my current assignment in the Church, I have learned another lesson relative to living the gospel today as opposed to dreaming about how I would have lived it in the time of the Prophet Joseph Smith. Soon after my call, I was assigned to visit conferences at the Rochester New York Stake and the Rochester New York Palmyra Stake, both of which would be held on the same weekend. I was excited with the possibility of going to the Hill Cumorah, the Sacred Grove, and other sites in our early Church history. I had seen these places before but not since this call. To do so, I would have to leave a day early, on Thursday rather than Friday afternoon. That would be all right—except that the Presiding Bishopric meets with the First Presidency at eight o'clock every Friday morning. However, since I would be attending almost twice the usual number of meetings on my assignment, I reasoned that I should leave earlier. With this rationalization, I left Thursday afternoon and arrived in Rochester late that night.

Early Friday morning I went to the Sacred Grove and walked straight up the path. As I entered the grove I noticed that I was alone. It was March 29, 1986, a day similar to that day in the spring of 1820 when Joseph Smith had entered the grove: "a beautiful, clear day." (JS–H 1:14.)

As I sat down and read the Joseph Smith story, I experienced basically what I had hoped for—a beautiful feeling of the reality of the events as recorded by Joseph. I thought how sacred this ground was, and the thought came to my mind: If Joseph were allowed to come to the Sacred Grove today and to sit down on the log next to me, what would he tell me? In the Doctrine and Covenants we read how the Lord sometimes told Joseph, in essence, "Tell my servant Sydney Rigdon to do this," and "Tell my servant Oliver Cowdery to do that." If Joseph were allowed to come and give me a revelation, I wondered, what would it be? "Tell my servant Glenn Pace to . . ."

Then I received a message, one that I will try to put in scriptural language, although it is not scripture except to me. It was something like this: "Why seek ye the Prophet Joseph Smith in the Sacred Grove this morning when, at this very hour, before the Prophet Ezra Taft Benson sits your empty chair?"

This was a sobering thought! I realized that it is easy to get caught up in history and even in the beauty of what it feels like to have a testimony and let it end there. A testimony becomes meaningful only when it leads to action—to living the gospel.

In summary, it is incumbent upon every member of the Church to obtain a testimony of the gospel. We cannot move forward to the next plateau on the testimony of another person. Obtaining a testimony is relatively easy for an honest seeker of the truth, for by studying, praying, and living gospel principles, each one has access to the undeniable witness of the Spirit.

Retaining a testimony is a little harder because once we have received a witness, we must do something about it. Many individuals who receive a testimony become lost along the way because they wander into forbidden paths. Others fail to continue progressing spiritually because they cling to their own abilities and will not make a leap of faith. Still others fail to use their own innate abilities and wait to be miraculously carried to a greater vista without exerting any effort of their own. Either of the latter groups can become disenchanted and frustrated. As a result, they can drift into sitting on the sidelines and criticizing those who are using their best spiritual and physical attributes to move the kingdom forward.

The time must come when each of us will accept the reality of the Restoration and get on with it. This may mean we have to withhold judgment on some intellectual questions. It means we must overlook weaknesses in others who may be presiding over us on all levels, local or general.

How tragic it will be if we don't each come to grips with our own personal potential and learn the role the Lord has in mind for us. How sad if we waste one more day with a lack of commitment and not meet the measure of our creation. When we genuinely lay everything on the altar, an illumination follows that helps us understand what our role is to be in building God's kingdom today. When we accept the gospel as being a reality and lay our all on the altar, we are ready to move on to greater heights. Join me in the next section as we get up and leave the rest, relaxation, and beauty of the first plateau and begin our climb to the joys received on the second plateau. A testimony is simply not enough.

Second Plateau

Sanctification

6

What Does Sanctification Mean?

If we are not careful, we can make the obtaining and retaining of a testimony our whole objective. Once they have obtained a testimony, many people have a tendency to relax until they start to feel it slip; then they put forth additional effort in studying and praying. When they feel that familiar spirit once more, they breathe a sigh of relief and say to themselves, "Thank heavens, it's back" — and they begin to relax again. This cycle can repeat itself over and over again until they realize that a testimony is not the objective. Perfection and, consequently, exaltation is the goal toward which we should all be working.

A testimony that Joseph Smith saw God the Father and His Son, Jesus Christ, is only the beginning. What is important is what the Restoration means to you and me personally and individually, not the fact that we know that a third party, Joseph Smith, actually saw Deity. We have to arrive at that stage quickly so that the teachings of the gospel and its importance to us can begin to take deep root in our lives.

I have chosen to call the second plateau *sanctification*. Other names that might be used are purification, the mighty change, born again, or even converted.

President Marion G. Romney distinguished the difference between converted (born again) and having a testimony as follows:

"Webster says the verb *convert* means 'to turn from one belief or course to another'; that *conversion* is 'a spiritual and moral *change* attending a *change* of belief with conviction.' As used in the scriptures, *converted* generally implies not merely mental acceptance of Jesus and his teaching, but also a motivating faith in him and in his gospel—a faith which works a transformation, an actual *change*, in one's understanding of life's meaning and in his allegiance to God—in interest, in thought, and in conduct. While conversion may be accomplished in stages, one is not really converted in the full sense of the term unless and until he is at heart a new person. *Born again* is the scriptural term.

"In one who is wholly converted, desire for things inimical to the gospel of Jesus Christ has actually died, and substituted therefor is a love of God with a fixed and controlling determination to keep his commandments. . . .

"From some of the Savior's sayings, it would seem that there might even be people in high places whose conversion is not complete. For example, conversing with his apostles at his last supper, he said to Peter, 'Simon, Simon, behold Satan hath desired to have you, that he may sift you as wheat: But I have prayed for thee, that thy faith fail not: and when thou art converted, strengthen thy brethren.' (Luke 22:31–32.)

"From this it would appear that membership in the Church and conversion are not necessarily synonymous. Being converted, as we are here using the term, and having a testimony are not necessarily the same thing either. A testimony comes when the Holy Ghost gives the earnest seeker a witness of the truth. A moving testimony vitalizes faith—that is, it induces repentance and obedience to the commandments. Conversion, on the other hand, is the fruit of, or the reward for, repentance and obedience. (Of course, one's testimony continues to increase as he is converted.)" (*Look to God and Live*, 1971, pp. 108–9, 111.)

When we finally commit to living the gospel rather than merely maintaining a testimony of it, our spirits can begin a metamorphosis. Elder John A. Widtsoe wrote: "When there is harmony between the instrument and the pounding message, there is joy in the heart. The world's confusion roots in discord, lack of harmony. To be out of focus or to live in the midst of static is to be in semi-darkness and chaos. To have control of self, to bid the baser appetites depart, is to walk through life in full light and with full power. They who think the path difficult, have not tried it. 'Living the gospel' is the true way to the full and free expression of human powers, to the help that the Spirit of God can give.

"It may be added that all who yield to such obedience to God's law undergo a real transformation, by the Holy Ghost, which enables them more and more, to receive and understand spiritual messages. Unless that transformation is accomplished, a person is opaque to spiritual truth, and the 'things of God' are beyond his understanding." (*Evidences and Reconciliations*, p. 88.)

According to Elder Bruce R. McConkie, "By the power of the Holy Ghost — who is the Sanctifier (3 Ne. 27:19–21) — dross, iniquity, carnality, sensuality, and every evil thing is burned out of the repentant soul as if by fire; the cleansed person becomes literally a new creature of the Holy Ghost. (Mosiah 27:24–26.) He is born again." (*Mormon Doctrine*, Salt Lake City: Bookcraft, 1966, p. 73.)

In connection with this fine-tuning, Joseph Smith said: "We consider that God has created man with a mind capable of instruction, and a faculty which may be enlarged in proportion to the heed and diligence given to the light communicated from heaven to the intellect; and that the nearer man approaches perfection, the clearer are his views, and the greater his enjoyments, till he has overcome the evils of his life and lost every desire for sin; and like the ancients, arrives at that point of faith where he is wrapped in the power and glory of his Maker and is caught up to dwell with Him." (*Teachings of the Prophet Joseph Smith*, p. 51.)

Elder McConkie was very clear in differentiating between baptism and being born again: "Mere compliance with the formality of the ordinance of baptism does not mean that a person has been born again. No one can be born again without baptism, but the immersion in water and the laying on of hands to confer the Holy Ghost do not of themselves guarantee that a person has been or will be born again. The new birth takes place only for those who actually enjoy the gift or companionship of the Holy Ghost, only for those who are fully converted, who have given themselves without restraint to the Lord. Thus Alma addressed himself to his 'brethren of the church,' and pointedly asked them if they had 'spiritually been born of God,' received the Lord's image in their countenances, and had the 'mighty change' in their hearts which always attends the birth of the Spirit. (See Alma 5:14–31.)

"Those members of the Church who have actually been born again are in a blessed and favored state. They have attained their position, not merely by joining the Church, but through faith (1 John 5:1), righteousness (1 John 2:29), love (1 John 4:7), and overcoming the world. (1 John 5:4.)" (*Mormon Doctrine*, p. 101.)

The scriptures are full of examples of sanctification, purification, being born again, and the mighty change. I will quote just a few to demonstrate how extensively these subjects are taught. First, from the Bible:

"And I will give them one heart, and I will put a new spirit within you; and I will take the stony heart out of their flesh, and will give them an heart of flesh: That they may walk in my statutes, and keep mine ordinances, and do them: and they shall be my people, and I will be their God." (Ezekiel 11:19–20.)

"Many shall be purified, and made white, and tried; but the wicked shall do wickedly: and none of the wicked shall understand; but the wise shall understand." (Daniel 12:10.)

"Draw nigh to God, and he will draw nigh to you. Cleanse your hands, ye sinners; and purify your hearts, ye double minded." (James 4:8.)

"Seeing ye have purified your souls in obeying the truth through the Spirit unto unfeigned love of the brethren, see that ye love one another with a pure heart fervently." (1 Peter 1:22.)

"And every man that hath this hope in him purifieth himself, even as he is pure." (1 John 3:3.)

"We know that whosoever is born of God sinneth not; but he that is begotten of God keepeth himself, and that wicked one toucheth him not." (1 John 5:18.)

As is the case with most doctrine, the Book of Mormon is clearest on this issue as well:

"For the natural man is an enemy to God, and has been from the fall of Adam, and will be, forever and ever, unless he yields to the enticings of the Holy Spirit, and putteth off the natural man and becometh a saint through the atonement of Christ the Lord, and becometh as a child, submissive, meek, humble, patient, full of love, willing to submit to all things which the Lord seeth fit to inflict upon him, even as a child doth submit to his father." (Mosiah 3:19.)

"It came to pass that when Ammon arose he also administered unto them, and also did all the servants of Lamoni; and they did all declare unto the people the self-same thing—that their hearts had been changed; that they had no more desire to do evil." (Alma 19:33.)

"Nevertheless they did fast and pray oft, and did wax stronger and stronger in their humility, and firmer and firmer in the faith of Christ, unto the filling their souls with joy and consolation, yea, even to the purifying and the sanctification of their hearts, which sanctification cometh because of their yielding their hearts unto God." (Helaman 3:35.)

"Father, I thank thee that thou hast purified those whom I have chosen, because of their faith, and I pray for them, and also for them who shall believe on their words, that they may be purified in me, through faith on their words, even as they are purified in me." (3 Nephi 19:28.)

"Wherefore, . . . pray unto the Father with all the energy of heart, that ye may be filled with this love, which he hath bestowed upon all who are true followers of his Son, Jesus Christ; that ye may become the sons of God; that when he shall appear we shall be like him, for we shall see him as he is; that we may have this hope; that we may be purified even as he is pure." (Moroni 7:48.)

As we would expect, modern-day scripture continues to emphasize the importance of this doctrine:

"Ye are to be taught from on high. Sanctify yourselves and ye shall be endowed with power, that ye may give even as I have spoken." (D&C 43:16.)

"Now this Moses plainly taught to the children of Israel in the wilderness, and sought diligently to sanctify his people that they might behold the face of God." (D&C 84:23.)

"For whoso is faithful unto the obtaining these two priesthoods of which I have spoken, and the magnifying their calling, are sanctified by the Spirit unto the renewing of their bodies." (D&C 84:33.)

My favorite scriptural illustration is in Mosiah, when King Benjamin addressed the members of the church. After delivering his address, we are told, "he sent among them, desiring to know of his people if they believed the words which he had spoken unto them. And they all cried with one voice, saying: Yea, we believe all the words which thou hast spoken unto us; and also, we know of their surety and truth, because of the Spirit of the Lord Omnipotent, which has wrought a mighty change in us, or in our hearts, that we have no more disposition to do evil, but to do good continually." (Mosiah 5:1–2.)

In verse 2 of this scripture we see three types of testimonies:

1. "Yea, we believe all the words" (below the first plateau).

2. "We know of their surety and truth" (the first plateau).

3. "The Lord Omnipotent . . . has wrought a mighty change in us . . . that we have no more disposition to do evil, but to do good continually" (the second plateau).

There is a vast difference between *being* good and *doing* good. Imagine how free we would be if we were able to express our true feelings through our actions rather than restraining our actions to hide our true feelings?

We should all be striving for a disposition to do no evil, but to do good continually. This isn't a resolve or a discipline; it is a disposition. We do things because we want to, not just because we know we should. Enos had this experience:

"Behold, I went to hunt beasts in the forests; and the words which I had often heard my father speak concerning eternal life, and the joy of the saints, sunk deep into my heart. And my soul hungered; and I kneeled down before my Maker, and I cried unto him in mighty prayer and supplication for mine own soul; and all the day long did I cry unto him; yea, and when the night came I did still raise my voice high that it reached the heavens. And there came a voice unto me, saying: Enos, thy sins are forgiven thee, and thou shalt be blessed. And I, Enos, knew that God could not lie; wherefore, my guilt was swept away."

When Enos was told that this was accomplished because of the sacrifice of the Savior, he said, "Now, it came to pass that when I had heard these words I began to feel a desire for the welfare of my brethren, the Nephites; wherefore, I did pour out my whole soul unto God for them." The Lord told Enos He would personally visit the Nephites, and because of this outpouring of love, Enos said, "My faith began to be unshaken in the Lord; and I prayed unto him with many long strugglings for my brethren, the Lamanites." (Enos 1:3–6, 9, 11.)

In other words, Enos had such love for his fellowman that he was now praying for his enemies and even had genuine concern for them. This was not because he thought he should or that he had been so commanded, but because he wanted to. He had received a mighty change. His disposition was such that he felt a desire for the welfare of his brethren. He didn't say, "The Lord commanded me to worry about my brethren." He had a disposition to do good rather than just a discipline of doing good.

Sometimes we overlook the fact that a spiritual transformation or metamorphosis must take place within us. It comes about through grace and by the Spirit of God, although it does not come about until we have truly repented and proven ourselves worthy. We can be guilty of being so careful to live the letter of the law that we don't develop our inner spiritual nature and fine-tune our spiritual communication to the point that we may receive sanctification and purification. My conclusion is that we will not be saved by works if those works are not born of a disposition to do good, as opposed to an obligation to do good.

Sometimes we lose sight of the purpose of the Church or, for that matter, what the Church really is. What is the role of the Church in the sanctifying process?

In the Church, I fear, sometimes programs have triumphed over principles. It is easy to become captivated by programs and forget the principles. We can become so prolific and creative in our Church programs that we can lose track of our objective. Someone has said that a fanatic is one who, once having lost track of his objective, doubles his effort. We become so hypnotized by the form that we can't see the substance. The result is a shallowness in our spirituality. Programs blindly followed bring us to a discipline of doing good, but principles properly understood and practiced bring us to a disposition to do good.

What does the Church mean to you? Imagine it without beautiful buildings, banquets, plays, basketball, softball, Eagle Scouts, the Mormon Tabernacle Choir, Brigham Young University, beautiful flowers on Temple Square, Young Women medallions, Church magazines, canneries, seminary and super activities for the youth, Christmas lights on Temple Square, and so forth. If this list, and many more items that could be added, is what the Church means to us, we are failing in teaching the gospel. All of these things can be helpful, but they are only a means to an end.

As great as the various programs of the Church are, they carry with them a potential danger. If we are not careful, it is possible to get so wrapped up in the programs that we forget the principles. We can fall into the trap of mistaking traditions for principles and confusing programs with their objectives.

One Saturday morning, I was on my way to fulfill an assignment on a welfare farm. We were to clean the weeds out of an irrigation ditch. My route took me past the home of an elderly widow in my ward who was weeding her front yard. The temperature was already in the mid-eighties, and she looked as if she were close to having sunstroke. For a fleeting moment I thought I should stop and lend a helping hand, but my conscience allowed me to drive on because, after all, I hadn't been assigned to help her. My assignment was on the welfare farm.

I wonder what would have happened had I followed the spontaneous prompting of the Spirit and unleashed the genuine compassion I was feeling. I wonder what would have happened to her; I wonder what would have happened to me.

The early members of the Church had few of the things that we now supply for our members in so many programs, and yet thousands of them were willing to die for their beliefs—and many did. Do we have the spiritual depth they had? We do, but I fear it may be dormant. Could we have endured what they did with the testimony we now have? More importantly, can we go through that which is at our doorstep with the depth of spirituality we now possess?

7

Covenants and
Ordinances

By now I hope I have aroused within you, if you are not already there, a desire to move on to the second plateau. If so, you are asking yourself: What is it about the Church that brings a person to sanctification? How do I do it? It isn't so simple as deciding to pay your tithing, observe the Word of Wisdom, keep the Sabbath day holy, be morally clean, or any other of the disciplines the Lord has given us until such time as our disposition automatically has us act in the right manner. It isn't so simple as saying, "All right, I'm going to go get myself sanctified." It is similar to loving your neighbor as yourself: you can't get there by just gritting your teeth and charging forward.

No amount of rhetoric from me is going to bring this mighty change to *you*. And even if I have convinced you intellectually that it is something you should pursue, an intellectual decision is not enough. Feelings cannot be dictated by intellect. Christlike love is a gift of the Spirit. You will recall that the people in King Benjamin's time said, "The Spirit of the Lord Omnipotent . . . has wrought a mighty change in us." (Mosiah 5:2.) We are, therefore, dependent upon the Spirit to bring us to this condition.

It begins with faith, repentance, and the gift of the Holy Ghost. With faith in the Lord Jesus Christ, we are ready to place our burden of sin at His feet. As we go through life, each of us makes mistakes and transgresses. As we receive a testimony of the Savior, we feel much like Alma: "I was racked with eternal torment, for my soul was harrowed up to the greatest degree and racked with all my sins. Yea, I did remember all my sins and iniquities, for which I was tormented with the pains of hell; yea, I saw that I had rebelled against my God, and that I had not kept his holy commandments. . . . Oh, thought I, that I could be banished and become extinct both soul and body, that I might not be brought to stand in the presence of my God, to be judged of my deeds." (Alma 36:12–13, 15.)

While some may not have the same gravity of sins for which to repent, all have need of much repentance. While in this repentant spirit, Alma realized that through the Atonement he could be forgiven. This led to unspeakable joy: "And now, behold, when I thought this, I could remember my pains no more; yea, I was harrowed up by the memory of my sins no more. And oh, what joy, and what marvelous light I did behold; yea, my soul was filled with joy as exceeding as was my pain! Yea, I say unto you, my son, that there could be nothing so exquisite and so bitter as were my pains. Yea, and again I say unto you, my son, that on the other hand, there can be nothing so exquisite and sweet as was my joy. Yea, methought I saw, even as our father Lehi saw, God sitting upon his throne, surrounded with numberless concourses of angels, in the attitude of singing and praising their God; yea, and my soul did long to be there." (Alma 36:19–22.)

At this point, we are baptized and receive the gift of the Holy Ghost. Subsequently, mistakes are made and the process repeats itself as we partake of the sacrament. As we accept the Savior and abide by the commandments, a metamorphosis of our spirit begins to take place. However, to bring us to ultimate sanctification, we need the higher ordinances, which are received in the temple. Becoming a Melchizedek Priesthood holder won't bring sanctification about. It is the ordinances of the Melchizedek Priesthood that bring this to pass. Hence, male and female alike receive the sanctifying power as they receive their endowments in the temple.

I am convinced that if the Saints really understood what can happen as a result of going to the temple, we would have a vast increase in the number of persons who hold temple recommends without sending anyone on a guilt trip. If a person wants to become sanctified, he or she must participate in the higher ordinances of the temple, receive the endowment given there, and remain true to the covenants made there.

In his dedicatory prayer of the Kirtland Temple, Joseph Smith explained the purpose of the temple. He said, in part: "And now, Holy Father, we ask thee to assist us, thy people, with thy grace, in calling our solemn assembly, that it may be done to thine honor and to thy divine acceptance; and in a manner that we may be found worthy, in thy sight, to secure a fulfilment of the promises which thou hast made unto us, thy people, in the revelations given unto us; that thy glory may rest down upon thy people, and upon this thy house, which we now dedicate to thee, that it may be sanctified and consecrated to be holy, and that thy holy presence may be continually in this house; and that all people who shall enter upon the threshold of the Lord's house may feel thy power, and feel constrained to acknowledge that thou hast sanctified it, and that it is thy house, a place of thy holiness. . . .

"And we ask thee, Holy Father, that thy servants may go forth from this house armed with thy power, and that thy name may be upon them, and thy glory be round about them, and thine angels have charge over them." (D&C 109:10–13, 22.)

Simply put, an infusion of the sanctifying Spirit comes to those who have gone to the temple that is not available to those who have only received the gift of the Holy Ghost.

Too often we look upon becoming worthy to go to the temple as the objective. The real blessings of temple attendance are the insights we receive there and the power that lingers with us after having been there. To those who keep their covenants, the sanctifier (the Holy Ghost) continues its work between visits as well as during the sessions.

So why go to the temple? First, the Lord has commanded it. This is very clear in modern revelation: "For behold, I reveal unto you a new and an everlasting covenant; and if ye abide not that covenant, then are ye damned; for no one can reject this covenant and be permitted to enter into my glory. For all who will have a blessing at my hands shall abide the law which was appointed for that blessing, and the conditions thereof, as were instituted from before the foundation of the world." (D&C 132:4–5.)

Joseph Smith said: "There are mansions for those who obey a celestial law, and there are other mansions for those who come short of the law, every man in his own order." (*History of the Church* 6:365.)

President Joseph Fielding Smith explained: "I do not care what office you hold in this Church, you may be an apostle, you may be a patriarch, a high priest, or anything else, and you cannot receive the fulness of the priesthood unless you go into the temple of the Lord and receive these ordinances of which the prophet speaks. No man can get the fulness of the priesthood outside the temple of the Lord." (*Elijah, the Prophet and His Mission*, Salt Lake City: Deseret Book, 1957, p. 46.)

In addition to going to the temple because we are commanded, we should also have a *desire* to participate. I am convinced that once we truly understand ordinances, covenants, and endowments, we will become anxious to go to the temple, making it unnecessary for God to command us to go.

The ordinances performed in the temple include baptism, washing, anointing, ordination, endowment, marriage, and sealing of children to parents. Elder James E. Talmage described the endowment as follows:

"*The Temple Endowment*, as administered in modern temples, comprises instruction relating to the significance and sequence of past dispensations, and the importance of the present as the greatest and grandest era in human history. This course of instruction includes a recital of the most prominent events of the creative period, the condition of our first parents in the Garden of Eden, their disobedience and consequent expulsion from that blissful abode, their condition in the lone and dreary world when doomed to live by labor and sweat, the plan of redemption by which the great transgression may be atoned, the period of the great apostasy, the restoration of the Gospel with all its ancient powers and privileges, the absolute and indispensable condition of personal purity and devotion to the right in present life, and a strict compliance with Gospel requirements. . . .

"With the taking of each covenant and the assuming of each obligation a promised blessing is pronounced, contingent upon the faithful observance of the conditions." (*The House of the Lord,* Salt Lake City: Deseret Book, 1968, pp. 83–84.)

One might ask, "What difference does it make whether I go to the temple? Isn't the important thing how I live and how I treat my fellowman?"

This is the same as asking, "What difference does it make if I am baptized and receive the Holy Ghost? Can't the Holy Ghost descend on me if I live righteously without the laying on of hands, and can't I be forgiven of my sins by repenting without being immersed in water?"

The answer to these questions is no. There exists an eternal truth that a certain process or outward manifestation is required before blessings can be received.

For example, when we were given the gift of the Holy Ghost, hands were placed upon our head and we received the companionship of the Holy Ghost. We can continue to receive it as long as we are faithful. We have complied with an ordinance and we know we received the gift.

We often speak of the "mantle" of a bishop. Those who have been bishops have felt it. Others have seen it descend upon a bishop and bring about a change in him. When does this happen? After he has been called and ordained. The ordination is necessary first.

In a like manner, there are blessings of the temple. When we receive those blessings, the Spirit begins to perfect us in ways not available to someone who has been baptized but not endowed. A new level of revelation becomes available to those who make—and keep—the covenants and who perform the ordinances of the temple. They begin to live by celestial laws and thereby receive celestial blessings. And as we return to the temple frequently, we bless the dead for whom we serve as proxy and we are blessed and strengthened for our obedience.

While the ordinances and covenants are required, it should be pointed out they are only the beginning. They give us the right to begin the journey to perfection. They give us access to spiritual gifts necessary to bring about perfection. However, it is through our obedience, sacrifice, and adherence to gospel principles that these gifts bear fruit.

In order to reach the highest degree of the celestial kingdom, it is necessary not only to receive the endowment but also to participate in the new and everlasting covenant of marriage. Adam said, "Therefore shall a man leave his father and his mother, and shall cleave unto his wife, and they shall be one flesh." (Abraham 5:18.) Paul noted: "Nevertheless neither is the man without the woman, neither the woman without the man, in the Lord." (1 Corinthians 11:11.) And in the Doctrine and Covenants we are told: "In the celestial glory there are three heavens or degrees; and in order to obtain the highest, a man must enter into this order of the priesthood [meaning the new and everlasting covenant of marriage]; and if he does not, he cannot obtain it." (D&C 131:1 – 3.)

Elder Widtsoe wrote: "Modern revelation sets forth the high destiny of those who are sealed for everlasting companionship. They will be given opportunity for a greater use of their powers. That means progress. They will attain more readily to their place in the presence of the Lord; they will increase more rapidly in every divine power; they will approach more nearly to the likeness of God; they will more completely realize their divine destiny. And this progress is not delayed until life after death. It begins here, today, for those who yield obedience to the law. Life is tasteless without progress. Eternal marriage, with all that it means, provides for unending advancement. 'Eternal increase' is the gift to all who enter into the eternal marriage covenant, as made in the temples of the Lord.

"They who have won a temple marriage have been sealed for time and eternity by the power of the Holy Priesthood. This is the supreme power committed to man's keeping. That power issues from the unseen world. It gives life and light to the world. Human life with its cares and worries is transfigured into a radiant experience and adventure when it clings to this divine power and is blessed by it. To walk under divine authority, to possess it, to be a part of it, is to walk with heads erect, with grateful hearts, before our fellow men and our Father in heaven. The men and women who have come with this power out of the Lord's holy house will be hedged about by divine protection and walk more safely among the perplexities of earth. They will be indeed the ultimate conquerors of earth, for they come with the infinite power of God to solve the problems of earth. Spiritual power accompanies all who marry in the temple, if they thenceforth keep their sacred covenants." (*Evidences and Reconciliations,* pp. 300–301.)

Why can't a person who isn't married obtain the highest degree of the celestial kingdom?

We are too quick to suggest, as the overriding reason, the ability to have children. Remember, the Father did not say, "It is not good for man not to be able to have children." The Father said, "It is not good that the man should be alone." (Genesis 2:18; see also Moses 3:18; Abraham 5:14.)

I would like to propose two reasons why the Lord's plan would be frustrated without the introduction of the male and female. The most obvious is parenthood. The second is less obvious but, in my opinion, more profound. It has to do with Eve's role in Adam's quest for individual exaltation, and vice versa.

I believe that the Father's statement that "it is not good that the man should be alone" had much deeper meaning than the obvious biological implications. It also went further than providing Adam with "company." Perhaps the reason why a person cannot enter the highest degree of the celestial kingdom without a companion is not because that person has not obeyed a celestial law, but because he or she hasn't become a celestial being. Is it possible there is a limit to our spiritual development so long as we are single? Is there a spiritual development that can be obtained only when a man and a woman join their incomplete selves into a complete couple through celestial marriage?

A man and a woman can accomplish marvelous things alone. However, they are incomplete until they are united physically, emotionally, psychologically, and, most importantly, spiritually. Also, when a man and a woman are joined together by anything short of the temple sealing, there is a limit to their progress no matter how compatible they are. Could it be that just as conception requires the union of male- and female-produced cells, perfection requires the spiritual union of the male and female?

We commonly hear the phrase "Men have the priesthood and women have been given the blessing of conceiving and bearing children." Without perfection, neither assignment meets the full measure of its creation. After perfection comes the ultimate role of god and goddess. Eternal roles, one complementing the other, one dependent upon the other. Perfection through the male and female spiritual union is dependent upon the sanctification process, which is a gift of the Spirit, available only to those in tune with that spirit and married under the covenant.

How I wish every priesthood holder would realize how absolutely dependent he is on his wife for his perfection and exaltation. Thankfully, many men do realize this. Unfortunately, however, some look upon the patriarchal order as a monarchal order. The patriarchal order is not an authority of command, but a point of order.

To the single women of the Church, this promise of a prophet, President Ezra Taft Benson, has been given (of course, the same promise would apply to worthy single men): "I also recognize that not all women in the Church will have an opportunity for marriage and motherhood in mortality. But if those of you in this situation are worthy and endure faithfully, you can be assured of all blessings from a kind and loving Heavenly Father—and I emphasize *all blessings*. I assure you that if you have to wait even until the next life to be blessed with a choice companion, God will surely compensate you. Time is numbered only to man. God has your eternal perspective in mind." (*Ensign*, November 1988, p. 97.)

In summary, sanctification is a gift of God and comes to those who qualify for it by performing the ordinances and making and keeping the covenants at baptism and in the temple.

8

The Trials
of Life

From a practical standpoint, after having received the covenants and ordinances, how does one consciously work toward sanctification? I offer six suggestions, all of which can occur simultaneously:

1. Take time one quiet morning or evening to take stock of yourself. Think of all the things the Church requires of you and place them in one of two categories: (a) I do it because I know I should, or (b) I do it because I want to. You may be surprised at how far along you are already. On the other hand, you may be very disappointed.

2. Read the scriptures. The Lord is not going to bless us with additional insights when we fail to take advantage of that which is already available to us. You might start by looking in the Topical Guide and reading scriptures on sanctification, purification, mighty change, born again, converted, consecration, and other related terms.

3. Keep the commandments. If necessary, keep them by faith alone at first. Keep them out of discipline. When Adam was asked why he offered up sacrifices, he said, "I know not, save the Lord commanded me." (Moses 5:6.) Great blessings come from obedience, even when we don't intellectually understand why. It is far better to keep the commandments out of discipline alone than not to keep them at all.

4. Always act on a genuine, warm impulse to do good. This can be as simple as an expression of appreciation, a note of encouragement, a visit to someone who is lonely, a compliment—anything that is positive and genuinely felt. Love feeds and expands on genuine acts of Christian service. As we act on these genuine impulses, they come more frequently and become stronger until we reach the point where our very disposition is to look for ways to serve others.

5. In your daily prayers, ask for sanctification. Ask the Lord to bring into your life those things which you need in order to place your spirit in a condition where it can be sanctified.

6. Use the heartaches and setbacks of life as stepping-stones to increased spirituality. If we react to setbacks and even tragedy by turning ourselves upward with a broken heart and contrite spirit, we place ourselves in a position where the sanctification process can accelerate geometrically.

The last point deserves some amplification. The key to the sanctification process lies in the way we respond to the adversities we face and the compassion we feel because of having been through these adversities. Compassion that we can gain in no other way develops within us when we have been through a trial. I am convinced that before the mighty change can occur within us, each of us will obtain a broken heart and a contrite spirit through experiences we receive in life.

I remember grasping this concept, in a very limited way, in my early high school years. I love sports. In grade school and junior high school, I dreamed of completing a pass in a football game with time running out, and thereby winning the state championship. I had similar fantasies regarding a last-second shot in basketball, and a home run in the bottom of the ninth inning in a baseball game.

As a sophomore in high school, because I had a small frame, I decided basketball was my game. I was quick and had a good two-handed set shot. (If you don't know what that is, ask someone over forty to tell you about it.) Tryouts were held in October. I played hard, stole the ball on several occasions, and made a few long, outside set shots; however, when the coach posted the names of the team members, my name was not on the list. I was crushed. My dream of having the cheerleaders swarm all over me after my game-winning shot was lost forever.

By the next summer I regrouped and decided maybe football was my game after all. At tryouts I put on a helmet, shoulder pads, and other gear. On my way out to the practice field, I remember looking in the mirror and saying to myself, "Hey, you look taller! And when you turn sideways, you don't disappear!" But then I noticed that the big guys looked bigger too.

In the first few drills, I felt fine. My speed allowed me to come in near the first in the sprints, and my confidence soared. Then came scrimmage. I was given the ball and told to run straight up the middle. As I got to the line, I was met by the biggest defensive lineman on the team. He planted his helmet in the pit of my stomach, wrapped his arms around my thighs, picked me up, threw me on the ground, and jumped on top of me. The only reason I didn't fumble was that the ball was implanted in my rib cage. As my friends carried my limp, breathless body off the field, I heard the coach say to the tackle, "Ooh! Wow! Nice hit, Kimber!"

Once again my dreams were shattered—not to mention my ribs and my ego. In the weeks that followed, I began to look around to see what else life had to offer. It took a while, but I made a marvelous discovery: there is a lot more to life than sports. I looked at my classmates in a different light. In addition to the respect I already had for good athletes, I began to appreciate the individual talents of each person. I marveled at those gifted with artistic ability. I looked at their paintings and thrilled at their talent. Others had developed their talents in music. I watched in amazement as a pianist played classical music. A dancer fascinated me with her grace and creativity. I read things written by a gifted poet. I laughed and cried as I watched some thespians perform. They actually made me forget who they were and convinced me they had become the characters on the stage. Some of my friends excelled in academics. And perhaps the most important talents are those we are likely to take for granted, such as compassion, benevolence, and integrity.

In short, a whole new world began to appear. I remember thinking how sad it was that talents such as these didn't receive the publicity and glory afforded athletic heroes. I thought of the hours, days, weeks, months, and years of practice, study, and meditation it took to develop such talents without having the encouragement of a cheering crowd.

I learned to appreciate and love a variety of friends. I also learned to feel genuine joy for their accomplishments—similar to the manner of Alma. He and Ammon separated as both left for their missions, and when they finally got back together after many years, Alma said: "God hath called me by a holy calling, to preach the word unto this people, and hath given me much success, in the which my joy is full. But I do not joy in my own success alone, but my joy is more full because of the success of my brethren. . . . Now, when I think of the success of these my brethren my soul is carried away, even to the separation of it from the body, as it were, so great is my joy." (Alma 29:13–14, 16.)

The disappointment I suffered relative to high school athletics softened my heart and increased my love and appreciation for a broad spectrum of friends at school.

With our limited understanding, we may wish life were easier. Sometimes we look at the nonmembers around us and envy their life-style. Several years ago I heard a popular song that contained the line "I'd rather laugh with the sinners than cry with the saints." My immediate reaction was anger. When I heard the song again, I laughed at myself because in the interim I had figured out why the line made me so mad. It was because it sounded so true!

In grade school, my parents made me go to church on Sunday while others went to the movies. In junior high school, I collected fast offerings on Sunday while others slept till noon. In high school, I passed up working on Sunday and earning double time at a grocery store so I could keep the Sabbath day holy. During my mission I walked down the streets on Saturday nights with my companion while others our age drove past us with their dates, laughing, pointing, and asking, "What's with those guys?"

As a young married couple, my wife and I attended church with our squirming children. On Super Bowl Sunday, while the rest of the world ate, drank, and cheered, we could be found pulling the hair and flipping the heads or ears of our children and encouraging them to listen to the words of a member of the stake high council. While traveling in our old clunker of a station wagon, we would pull up alongside a Mercedes Benz. The occupants, with their national average 1.7 kids dressed in designer jeans, would point and laugh at my six kids dressed in their Toughskins. That is why that line made me so mad!

My frustration over this issue peaked a few years ago when my older children prevailed in getting me to attend a concert at Brigham Young University. When the singer announced the song from which the following line is taken, "I'd rather laugh with the sinners than cry with the saints," the crowd went wild. He said, "I'm not trying to convert anyone—I just want to provide you with an alternative." I thought the roof was going to come off the place. I wanted to race down the steps, grab the microphone, and give my opinion on the subject. Of course, my children would have been horrified.

The statement "sinners laugh and saints cry" is a simplistic generalization at best. We Latter-day Saints definitely have our share of laughter, and some sinners leave a trail of broken lives and buckets of tears. For saints as well as sinners, all that is meaningful in life doesn't have to be funny. However, to brush aside the line in the song with this equally simplistic argument would be to ignore a reasonable question. At a given point in time, don't many who make no effort to live Church standards appear to be enjoying life more than some who do?

Our lives as Latter-day Saints may appear to be controlled by inhibitions, constraints, service, sacrifice, guilty consciences, and financial obligations. In the world we see people with none of these so-called restrictions—people who are home with their families on more than just Monday night and who have 10 to 15 percent more of their gross income to spend.

When our children were younger and we would be on our way to Sunday church meetings, occasionally we would pass a car pulling a boat. My children would become silent and press their noses against the windows and ask, "Dad, why can't we go waterskiing today instead of to church?" Sometimes I would take the easy but cowardly way out and answer, "It's simple: we don't have a boat." However, on my more conscientious days, I would muster up all the logic and spirituality available to a patriarch of a family and try to explain how much happier our family was because of our church activity.

I first realized I wasn't getting through when on a subsequent Sunday we saw a family laughing and excited as they loaded up their boat. One of my teenage sons said with a sly grin, "They're not really happy, huh, Dad?" That statement has become a family joke whenever we see someone doing something we cannot do. When I see a teenager driving a beautiful, expensive sports car, I say to my sons, "Now there's one miserable guy."

Our children are growing up in a most challenging and confusing world. Activities that have always been forbidden by the Lord and that for many years were frowned upon by society are now accepted and promoted by that same society. The media serve up these activities in such a fashion as to make them look very desirable. Add to acceptability and desirability the power of peer pressure, and you have an extremely explosive situation.

Lehi's vision of the tree of life is appropriate for our day. In that vision, he saw a great and spacious building, which represents the pride and temptations of the world: "It was filled with people, both old and young, . . . and their manner of dress was exceedingly fine; and they were in the attitude of mocking and pointing their fingers towards those who . . . were partaking of the fruit." (1 Nephi 8:27.)

Even though a person may have a testimony and want to do what is right, it is difficult not to be drawn to that great and spacious building. From all appearances, the people in the building look happy and free and seem to be having a great time. But don't mistake telestial pleasure for celestial happiness and joy. Don't mistake lack of self-control for freedom. Complete freedom without appropriate restraint makes people slaves to their appetites. Don't envy a lesser and lower life.

When I was in junior high school, I would get out of bed on cold winter mornings and head for the heat vent to get warm. The family cat would always beat me there, so I would gently shoo her away and sit down. Soon my mother would tell me it was time to leave for school. I would look out at the icicles on the house and dread going out into the cold, let alone beginning another day of school.

As I kissed my mother good-bye and went out the door, I would look longingly at my comfortable spot in front of the heat vent and find that the cat had repossessed it. How

I envied that cat! If that weren't enough, she would look up at me with heavy eyelids and an expression that seemed to laugh at me and say, "Have fun in school, Glenn. I'm sure glad I'm not a human." I hated it when she did that.

However, an interesting thing would happen as the day went on. I would come home after experiencing the joys and sorrows of the school day and see that lazy cat still curled up in front of the vent, and I would smile and say to her, "I'm sure glad I'm not a cat."

To those who are inching their way closer and closer to that great and spacious building, let me make it completely clear that the people in that building have absolutely nothing to offer except instant, short-term gratification that is inescapably connected to long-term sorrow and suffering. The commandments we observe have not been given by a dispassionate God to prevent us from having fun, but by a loving Father in Heaven who wants us to be happy while we are living on this earth as well as in the hereafter.

Compare the blessings of living the Word of Wisdom with those available if we choose to party with the individuals in the great and spacious building. Compare the joy of intelligent humor and wit with drunken, silly, crude, loud laughter. Compare our faithful, virtuous young women who still have a blush in their cheeks with those who, having long lost their blush, try to persuade others to join them in their loss. Compare lifting people up to putting people down. Compare the ability to receive personal revelation and direction in your life with being tossed to and fro with every wind of doctrine.

The members of many churches in the world have been putting pressure on their leaders to change doctrine to fit changing life-styles. Many such movements have been successful, and increasingly we see churches made up of the doctrines of men. However, there are absolute truths of eternity. They do not change as a society drifts from them. No popular vote can change an absolute, eternal truth. Legalizing an act does not make it moral. Don't be fooled by the argument "Everybody's doing it." Our spirits should be offended and our intelligences insulted by such reasoning.

When all of the evidence is in, the world's graduate school of hard knocks will teach what we learned in the kindergarten of our spiritual training: "Wickedness never was happiness." (Alma 41:10.) Why wait for finite man to prove what his infinite Creator has already revealed to His prophets?

9

Crying with the Saints

In spite of our knowledge that wickedness never was happiness, many tears are shed by Saints who are living the gospel, while laughter seems more prominent in the lives of those living a rather worldly life. The celestial happiness we seek does not come without effort. The voguish phrase "no pain, no gain" applies equally well to the things of the Spirit. Sometimes in the midst of trials we cry out, "What have I done wrong to deserve this?" Often, tribulation comes into our lives not because we are doing something wrong but because of what we are doing right.

In striving for the purification and sanctification that will lead us to exaltation, we all must pass through a certain amount of fire so that our spirits will be pliable in the hands of the Lord. Joseph Smith's life exemplifies this principle. There was probably not a darker period in his life, by all outward standards, than the winter of 1838–39 when he was imprisoned in Liberty Jail. The Saints were being persecuted, robbed, and murdered, and there was dissension and apostasy in their ranks.

We may be inclined to underestimate Joseph's suffering. I don't speak of the coldness of the jail, but of his discouragement. We may think that his anguish would be mitigated by his memory of having seen the Father and the Savior and by his memory of visits from Moroni, John the Baptist, Peter, James, John, and a host of other heavenly messengers. In reality, this knowledge may have intensified the pain. After all, Joseph had a perfect knowledge that God could free him.

It was in this setting that Joseph cried unto the Lord, "O God, where art thou? And where is the pavilion that covereth thy hiding place?" To this agonized plea came the Lord's answer: "My son, peace be unto thy soul; thine adversity and thine afflictions shall be but a small moment." (D&C 121:1, 7.) Then He added, "Know thou, my son, that all these things shall give thee experience, and shall be for thy good." (D&C 122:7.)

"For thy good"? What possible good could come from that experience? Elder B. H. Roberts gave an insight about the possible good that could come from such an experience when he described Joseph's reaction to a similar experience in 1842: "What is most pleasing to record of this period of enforced seclusion while avoiding his enemies, is the development of that tenderness of soul manifested in his reflections upon the friends who had stood by him from the commencement of his public career. . . . No act of kindness seems to go unmentioned. No risk run for him that is not appreciated. Indeed he gathers much benefit from those trials, since their effect upon his nature seems to be a softening rather than a hardening influence; and the trials of life are always beneficial where they do not harden and brutalize men's souls; and every day under his trials the Prophet seems to have grown more tender-hearted, more universal in his sympathies; his moments of spiritual exaltation are superb. No one can read them and doubt that the inspiration of God was giving this man's spirit understanding." (*History of the Church* 5:xxviii.)

Joseph taught, "The nearer we get to our heavenly Father, the more we are disposed to look with compassion on perishing souls; we feel that we want to take them upon our shoulders, and cast their sins behind our backs. . . . If you would have God have mercy on you, have mercy on one another." (*Teachings of the Prophet Joseph Smith*, p. 241.)

After the Lord told Joseph, "These things shall give thee experience, and shall be for thy good," He explained, "The Son of Man hath descended below them all. Art thou greater than he?" (D&C 122:8.)

Part of the reason the Savior suffered in Gethsemane was so that He would have infinite compassion for us as we experience our trials and tribulations. Through His suffering in Gethsemane, He became qualified to be the perfect judge. Not one of us will be able to approach Him on the Judgment Day and say, "You don't know what it was like." He knows the nature of our trials better than we do, for He "descended below them all."

As a loving Father in Heaven viewed His Beloved Son suffering in the Garden of Gethsemane, the Savior cried out, "O my Father, if it be possible, let this cup pass from me: nevertheless not as I will, but as thou wilt." (Matthew 26:39.)

Can you imagine the tears in the eyes of the Father when He had to deny His Son's request? Can you comprehend the sacred tears shed by the Father when He had to abandon the Savior on the cross and hear Him say, "My God, my God, why hast thou forsaken me"? (Mark 15:34.) And yet, even as God the Father and His Son Jesus Christ wept, sinners laughed.

Each of us must pass through our own gethsemanes. Ella Wheeler Wilcox wrote a poem titled "Gethsemane":

> In golden youth when seems the earth
> A Summer-land of singing mirth,
> When souls are glad and hearts are light,
> And not a shadow lurks in sight,
> We do not know it, but there lies
> Somewhere veiled under evening skies
> A garden which we all must see—
> The garden of Gethsemane.
>
> With joyous steps we go our ways,
> Love lends a halo to our days;
> Light sorrows sail like clouds afar,
> We laugh, and say how strong we are.
> We hurry on; and hurrying, go
> Close to the border-land of woe,
> That waits for you, and waits for me—
> Forever waits Gethsemane.
>
> Down shadowy lanes, across strange streams,
> Bridged over by our broken dreams;
> Behind the misty caps of years,
> Beyond the great salt fount of tears,
> The garden lies. Strive as you may,
> You cannot miss it in your way.
> All paths that have been, or shall be,
> Pass somewhere through Gethsemane.

All those who journey, soon or late,
Must pass within the garden's gate;
Must kneel alone in darkness there,
And battle with some fierce despair.
God pity those who can not say,
"Not mine but thine," who only pray,
"Let this cup pass," and cannot see
The *purpose* in Gethsemane.

There is probably no greater gethsemane for saint or sinner than the death of a child. Just minutes after he learned of his ten-year-old daughter's accidental death, a father I know wrote a letter to her. Note how this good man's gethsemane became a sanctifying experience because of his knowledge of the gospel and the gift he had received of the Comforter. Contrast his reaction with what it might have been without the light of the gospel:

If you may be permitted to listen, these are some thoughts your "Dear Ole Dad" would like to express in his and your mom's hour of joy and sorrow.

You have been an angel of light in our home. Even in your passing you have sanctified the experience by the sweet sorrow of this temporary parting. As I sit in this hotel room many miles from home and only moments after hearing of your passing, I have confidence that you are really home. It's pleasing to know that you are no longer encumbered by the mild but troublesome physical limitations you accepted and lived with in such an adorable, noncomplaining way.

Mom and I and your seven brothers and sisters are better because you came to our house. Soon after your day of birth you helped us to accept fear and the unknown; to better love others with physical, emotional, or mental challenges; to accept the disappointment accompanying an unknown prognosis; and to query and plead with our Father, who today you know better than we do. As you grew older, we learned determination from you, who had every right to spill your milk but never did, who royally beat your mom and dad in tetherball, who averaged 97 percent in spelling for an entire year and by sheer grit struggled with math, and who without ever a complaint sat with your mom every night—summer and school months—to read and understand what you had read. Yes, we did our best to help you learn, but what we learned from you cannot be printed in books—cannot be written—because it is almost too sacred to rehearse.

We pray for all of us whom the Lord expects to stay here on the job for yet a while. Our prayers are that we will be worthy to be reunited with you and to see you whole and perfect. Oh, how we would have loved to have you stay. How we would love to hear your ever-so-spontaneous "I love you." How we'd thrill to feel that clinging embrace. Oh yes, especially today.

I witnessed an explosion of sanctification one Sunday evening. My cousin called and asked me to join him at the hospital. His nineteen-year-old daughter had just been killed in an automobile accident. His wife arrived a few minutes after I did. He told her their daughter was gone, and for a few moments they stood over the lifeless body. The next day I wrote this letter to them expressing my feelings on that sacred, sanctifying experience:

Never have I felt more inadequate and helpless than when I walked into that hospital room made sacred by the passing of your beloved daughter—to see the pain on your faces and know I couldn't ease it. All I could do is what many others are doing, and that is to reach out to you with my love and support. Few of us have had the experience you are going through, but all of us have had tragedies of one kind or another and, therefore, feel the pain to some degree. Please accept our willingness to share yours with you.

I don't know why you chose to have me join you at that personal and sacred moment. For me, the time of death has held the same reverence as birth and temple marriage. After last night, I am feeling that it surpasses all others. I am grateful and humbled for the testimony I saw in you. Yes, there were tears, bewilderment, sorrow, regrets, and shock. However, overshadowing those emotions was something I will remember long after that memory fades. The Savior allowed me to see through spiritual eyes something easily missed under such trying conditions.

This was a zero hour in your spiritual preparedness. At such moments all facades fall from your being. There is nothing of this world to protect you. Lip service to the gospel would leave your souls completely unprotected. It was a day of spiritual reckoning. How did you do? Let me try to do justice to what I saw.

Above the tears, pain, and questions of why and how this accident could have been avoided, I saw dignity and majesty in both of you. I saw humble submission to the Lord; and through that humility and willingness to accept this tragedy without cursing God, you have earned the love God has for Abraham just as surely as if He had asked for your daughter's life. Very few of us will be asked to give our lives for the kingdom, but all of us must be willing to do so before we will be worthy of it. You have gone one step further. You have given something much dearer to you. Who of us would not gladly give our own life in place of our beloved children?

I can tell you that because of your acceptance and trust in our Father in Heaven, you have proven yourselves herewith. In short, I saw in you a god and a goddess, a king and a queen. I saw radiance emerge victorious from your countenances.

You have probably asked yourselves a thousand times: Is it because of something we did or didn't do that she was taken? Is it because we need an incentive to be better people? Perhaps it isn't what you need, but rather what the Lord needs from her in the world beyond.

You may cry because her early exit prevents her from the accomplishments of this life. Your hearts might ache for the grandchildren you would have loved; the births, baptisms, ordinations, and marriages. These events have not been taken from her or you, only delayed for a very short season. For her, the pain and suffering most of us will know when we approach death a moment at a time have been canceled. She will not see herself grow old. She will not be lonely in her old age. She will not experience what you are enduring right now. The negative experiences of life have been waived, but she will still have the privilege of participating in the positive experiences.

Therefore, we need not feel sorrow for her. She is with those she has known who have already passed through the veil. She is with those whom you have known and loved and whom she has never met. She has already made new friends. She is well and happy.

The sorrow you feel is for yourselves and those who are left behind, all of whom will join her one by one — some perhaps in months, others in years or decades. Don't feel guilty for your "self sorrow." How pathetic it would be if we didn't miss those who precede us in death. How empty our lives would be if the death of those close to us didn't bring unbearable pain. And yet, He who loves you for your love of Him will hold you up and nurse you back to a state of normalcy.

You will not forget her but you will love each other more, and the rest of your children will be closer than ever before. In this fashion she is doing her part to make certain you will be with her when your times come. She will not be disinterested in the family, although her new assignments will keep her busy.

Since my call as a General Authority, my responsibilities have taken me away from my family more than ever before. But my family has become dearer to me the more I serve in my assignment. In your daughter's case, travel is not a problem. As you recall, I was not able to perform her marriage because of an assignment out of town. We have restrictions here which do not saddle those who have passed on.

Even last night, in my mind's eye, I saw her enter the room where we were with her vacated body to do what she could to comfort you and then ask Grandpa and Grandma [who had both passed away earlier] to stay with us as she watched over her husband and the others who were hurt in the accident. It is incomprehensible that the family would become secondary to any assignment in the spirit world and, therefore, I can promise you that you will feel her spirit on those special family occasions, including this very time.

Thank you for showing me a righteous, dignified, eternal couple last night. Thank you for sharing the most sacred moment of your lives thus far. With you, I thank God for the knowledge He has given us. Please accept this feeble attempt to share this burden with you, thereby trying to make it lighter for you.

As we shed tears in our own gethsemanes while others laugh with the sinners, we must not curse the purifying fire in which we have been placed. Our crucible is divine and will ultimately sanctify and perfect us. Latter-day Saints don't seek the unpleasant things of life. We don't look for pain and suffering. However, we recognize that trials and tribulations come to all of us, and they can be turned into spiritual stepping-stones to sanctification and exaltation.

While on my mission, I received word that a friend had drowned. He was ice-skating on Utah Lake and fell through. About two years later his best friend also drowned in Utah Lake while saving the life of a young woman. Both boys were from my ward. I was home from my mission by then and went to the viewing. I had lived in the ward most of my life and knew both families well. The father of the second boy had been my bishop when I went on my mission. As my turn came to pay respects to the parents, I embraced each of them, shed tears with them, and shared experiences I had had with their son. I felt love and sympathy for them and expressed it as best I could.

As I moved on to the casket, I glanced back and witnessed a sacred scene I will never forget. Behind me in the line were the parents of the first boy. They said very little as they shed tears and embraced, much as I had done. However, they reached a place in the souls of the grieving parents I was unable to reach. They made a connection. They administered a soothing comfort of which I was incapable. They completely understood and had compassion and empathy. I hold that moment sacred.

We don't all have to suffer the *same thing* in order to develop that compassion which accompanies the mighty change, but we all must experience *something*. Although we might choose otherwise, we all must pass through a certain amount of trial and tribulation before we will humble ourselves to the point that our spirits can be molded by our Father in Heaven. "My people must needs be chastened until they learn obedience, if it must needs be, by the things which they suffer." (D&C 105:6.)

Orson F. Whitney wrote: "No pain that we suffer, no

trial that we experience is wasted. It ministers to our education, to the development of such qualities as patience, faith, fortitude and humility. All that we suffer and all that we endure, especially when we endure it patiently, builds up our characters, purifies our hearts, expands our souls, and makes us more tender and charitable, more worthy to be called the children of God . . . and it is through sorrow and suffering, toil and tribulation, that we gain the education that we come here to acquire and which will make us more like our Father and Mother in heaven." (Quoted by Spencer W. Kimball, "Tragedy or Destiny," *Improvement Era*, March 1966, p. 211.)

George Q. Cannon discussed the purifying nature of trials and tribulations as follows: "Whatever fate may threaten us, there is but one course for men of God to take, that is, to keep inviolate the holy covenants they have made in the presence of God and angels. For the remainder, whether it be life or death, freedom or imprisonment, prosperity or adversity, we must trust in God. We may say, however, if any man or woman expects to enter into the Celestial Kingdom of our God without making sacrifices and without being tested to the very utmost, they have not understood the Gospel. If there is a weak spot in our nature, or if there is a fiber that can be made to quiver or to shrink, we may rest assured that it will be tested. Our own weaknesses will be brought fully to light, and in seeking for help the strength of our God will also be made manifest to us." (*Gospel Truth*, p. 304.)

"The Lord our God is working with us; He is trying us, probably with trials of a new sort that He may approve of us in every respect. If we have set out to obtain celestial glory, the precious and inestimable gift of eternal lives, there is no trial necessary for our purification and perfection as Saints of God that we will not have to meet, contend with and overcome. Such trials will come in various shapes, on the right hand and on the left, whether they be in having everything move on prosperously, or in adversity, hardship and the laying down of our lives for the truth, until the design is fully accomplished and the dross of our natures is purified and these earthly tabernacles are redeemed from everything that is groveling and low and brought into entire subjection to the mind and will of God." (Ibid., p. 527.)

President Howard W. Hunter addressed this issue as he spoke in general conference about the troubles he was facing:

"Life—every life—has a full share of ups and downs. Indeed, we see many joys and sorrows in the world, many changed plans and new directions, many blessings that do not always look or feel like blessings, and much that humbles us and improves our patience and our faith. We have all had those experiences from time to time, and I suppose we always will.

"A passage from one of the greatest prophetic sermons ever given—King Benjamin's masterful discourse to the people of Zarahemla in the Book of Mormon—reads this way:

" 'Men drink damnation to their own souls except they humble themselves and become as little children. . . . For the natural man is an enemy to God, and has been from the fall of Adam, and will be, forever and ever, unless he yields to the enticings of the Holy Spirit, and putteth off the natural man and becometh a saint through the atonement of Christ the Lord, and becometh as a child, submissive, meek, humble, patient, full of love, willing to submit to all things which the Lord seeth fit to inflict upon him, even as a child doth submit to his father' (Mosiah 3:18–19).

"Being childlike and submitting to our Father's will is not always easy. President Spencer W. Kimball, who knew a good deal about suffering, disappointment, and circumstances beyond his control, once wrote: 'Being human, we would expel from our lives physical pain and mental anguish and assure ourselves of continual ease and comfort, but if we were to close the doors upon sorrow and distress, we might be excluding our greatest friends and benefactors. Suffering can make saints of people as they learn patience, long-suffering, and self-mastery' (*Faith Precedes the Miracle* [Salt Lake City: Deseret Book, 1972], p. 98).

"In that statement, President Kimball refers to closing doors upon certain experiences in life. That image brings to mind a line from Cervantes' great classic, *Don Quixote,* that has given me comfort over the years. In that masterpiece, we find the short but very important reminder that where one door closes, another opens. Doors close regularly in our lives, and some of those closings cause genuine pain and heartache. But I *do* believe that where one such door closes, another opens (and perhaps more than one), with hope and blessings in other areas of our lives that we might not have discovered otherwise.

"Our beloved quorum president, Marion G. Romney, . . . has known considerable pain and discouragement and has seen his plans changed during these past few years. But it was he who, from this very pulpit a few years ago, said that all men and women, including the most faithful and loyal, would find adversity and affliction in their lives because, in the words of Joseph Smith, 'Men have to suffer that they may come upon Mount Zion and be exalted above the heavens' (*History of the Church,* 5:556; see Conference Report, Oct. 1969, p. 57).

"President Romney then said: 'This does not mean that we crave suffering. We avoid all we can. However, we now know, and we all knew when we elected to come into mortality, that we would here be proved in the crucible of adversity and affliction. . . . [Furthermore,] the Father's plan for proving [and refining] his children did not exempt the Savior himself. The suffering he undertook to endure, and which he did endure, equaled the combined suffering of all men [and women] everywhere. Trembling and bleeding and wishing to shrink from the cup, he said, "I partook and finished my preparations unto the children of men" (D&C 19:18–19)' (in Conference Report, Oct. 1969, p. 57).

"These lines from Robert Browning Hamilton, titled 'Along the Road,' . . . teach a lesson on pleasure and a lesson on sorrow:

> "I walked a mile with Pleasure;
> She chattered all the way,
> But left me none the wiser
> For all she had to say.
> I walked a mile with Sorrow,
> And ne'er a word said she;
> But oh, the things I learned from her
> When Sorrow walked with me!"
> (*Ensign,* November 1987, pp. 54, 59.)

Elder Franklin D. Richards of the First Quorum of the Seventy once said: "Although it is not customary for one to seek out the difficult or unpleasant experiences, it is true that the trials and tribulations of life that stand in the way of man's growth and development become stepping-stones by which he climbs to greater heights, providing, of course, that he does not permit them to discourage him." (*Ensign*, December 1971, p. 50.)

As we petition the Lord that we might have this mighty change, we need to let the trials and tribulations that have come or may yet come into our lives propel us to this second plateau. We need to beware of self pity and, even worse, cursing the Lord for the situation in which we find ourselves. If we do not approach our individual problems with the right attitude, these stepping-stones become stumbling blocks and we may even fall to a lower plateau.

I know of no great person who has not had his or her share of adversity. We all have our own personal bag of rocks we are carrying around. Each one is different from every other one, and my load may not look too heavy to you and vice versa. I do know that we are each generally hit in an area that hurts us most. I also know that some of the biggest wounds we carry are self-inflicted and, in many cases, come to us as a result of transgression. Even the agony of transgression, however, can result in our sanctification when we truly repent and have a broken heart and contrite spirit.

I also know that the easiest way to lighten our load is to reach down and help carry someone else's. There is no greater cure for our own wounds than to dress the wounds of someone else.

While I have been speaking of tears of sorrow and pain shed by the saints, I would also suggest that the saints shed tears of joy during their sojourn on the earth. These tears are unique to saints and will never be shed by sinners.

When I was in an elders quorum presidency, we worked with several less-active families. In a personal interview with one couple, I asked, "Isn't it about time you went to the temple with your family?"

I couldn't believe their answer. They said, "Yes." We cried.

They were asked to speak about their "conversion" in a Saturday evening session of stake conference, and as they expressed their love, I cried. I thought I was all cried out by the time we went to the temple—until I saw them and their beautiful daughters kneel at the altar and be sealed for time and eternity.

A few years ago, President Ezra Taft Benson stood before the General Authorities in their monthly temple meeting. He had been ill, and it was the first time we had been together with him for several months. He expressed his love to us and said, "Brethren, it is so good to be with you again." And then the Prophet cried.

When the Savior concluded His visit to the people of Nephi, He felt their love and faith and was deeply touched. He had just announced that He must leave, but as He looked at the people, He "beheld they were in tears, and did look steadfastly upon him as if they would ask him to tarry a little longer with them. And he said unto them: Behold, my bowels are filled with compassion towards you."

Then Jesus healed the sick, and those who were healed did "bow down at his feet, and did worship him; and . . . did bathe his feet with their tears." And He "commanded that their little children should be brought. So they brought their little children and set them down upon the ground round about him."

After praying to the Father for the people, Jesus told them, "Blessed are ye because of your faith. And now behold, my joy is full." And then "he wept, . . . and he took their little children, one by one, and blessed them, and prayed unto the Father for them. And when he had done this he wept again." (3 Nephi 17:5–6, 10–12, 20–22.)

Elder Bruce R. McConkie spoke of tears in general conference just a few weeks before his death. In one of the most powerful testimonies I have ever heard, that special witness, who had full and complete knowledge that his passing was near, said: "I testify that [Jesus Christ] is the Son of the Living God and was crucified for the sins of the world. He is our Lord, our God, and our King. This I know of myself independent of any other person. I am one of his witnesses, and in a coming day I shall feel the nail marks in his hands and in his feet and shall wet his feet with my tears." (Conference Report, April 1985, p. 12.)

Those of us who witnessed the delivery of that magnificent address can testify that tears were flowing even as Elder McConkie stood at the pulpit. They were not tears of sorrow, but tears of joy at the anticipation of the blessing awaiting him.

Just one day before Elder McConkie's address, I had received my call to the Presiding Bishopric. One day after his address, at five o'clock on Easter morning, I was writing my remarks to be delivered that afternoon. As I reflected on his beautiful oration, I was overcome with the knowledge of my weaknesses and inadequacies. However, as I began to comprehend what had taken place in my own life, self-doubt was replaced with peace, confidence, and eternal joy. I wept. I penned these words, which seem appropriate to repeat at this time: "I love the Lord Jesus

Christ. I love the transformation his atonement has wrought in me. . . . I once was in darkness, and now see light. I once lost all of my confidence, and now know all things are possible in the Lord. I once felt shame and now am 'filled with his love, even unto the consuming of my flesh' (2 Ne. 4:21). 'I am encircled about eternally in the arms of his love' (2 Ne. 1:15)." (Conference Report, April 1985, p. 100.)

I feel the same way now as I did on that Easter Sunday. That knowledge brings tears.

Would I rather laugh with the sinners than cry with the saints? Not for one moment. Once one has felt the joy of the gospel, there is no going back into a frivolous world. Try as we may, travel where we may, there is an emptiness that all the laughter the world has to offer cannot fill. That emptiness can be filled only by placing ourselves in tune with eternal truths and living according to the prescribed laws of God.

As our understanding increases, we realize that tears of sorrow can be exquisitely beautiful—and that they ultimately give way to tears of eternal joy. In life, with all of its complications, we shed tears of both joy and sorrow. Those who react positively to life's challenges go through a refinement that propels them toward the second plateau.

10

The Savior's Example

The closer we get to sanctification, the nearer the Lord comes to us. We find ourselves literally coming unto Christ. With this perspective, we can begin to appreciate His life and why He was so selfless. We begin to appreciate that He is happy only when serving others. He understands the great principle and is an example of how one who has become sanctified acts and feels.

Lately I have been pondering the complete and absolute selflessness, or unselfishness, of the Savior. Sometimes we speak of Gethsemane and the crucifixion as being the example of His love for and His gift to us. Of course, this is His ultimate gift. I am thankful, however, that we know more about the Savior than just how He was born and how He died.

As I have studied *Jesus the Christ* by James E. Talmage,

my mind and heart have been turned to the life He lived rather than the death He suffered. I have also concentrated more on what He did rather than what He said. I have become more impressed with what He did on the way to deliver the Sermon on the Mount than with what He said in the sermon. The Savior's every thought and action were directed to the benefit of others. Even before He came to this earth, His work was "to bring to pass the immortality and eternal life of man." (Moses 1:39.)

We have all heard this scripture from the Pearl of Great Price quoted on numerous occasions. An insight into the Lord's unselfishness is gained by studying the verses preceding this verse. The scripture is part of a marvelous revelation wherein Moses was shown some sacred and mind-expanding realities, the first of which was to see Jesus Christ Himself in His spiritual form. "And he saw God [Jehovah] face to face, and he talked with him, and the glory of God was upon Moses; therefore Moses could endure his presence." (Moses 1:2.) Moses learned Jehovah was a man.

After revealing Himself to Moses, the Lord showed him this world. Soon Satan came and tried to convince Moses to worship him as the god of this earth. Moses passed the test by saying, "I will not cease to call upon God, I have other things to inquire of him: for his glory has been upon me, wherefore I can judge between him and thee. Depart hence, Satan." (Moses 1:18.)

The Lord then showed Moses incomprehensible creations and glories that could be understood only under the influence of the Spirit: "Moses cast his eyes and beheld the earth, yea, even all of it; and there was not a particle of it which he did not behold, discerning it by the spirit of God. And he beheld also the inhabitants thereof, and there was not a soul which he beheld not; and he discerned them by the Spirit of God; and their numbers were great, even numberless as the sand upon the sea shore." (Moses 1:27–28.)

This must have been overwhelming to Moses, and he wondered about the purpose of it all. Seemingly, the Lord teased him a little and didn't give him a direct answer to his thoughts. He said, "For mine own purpose have I made these things. Here is wisdom and it remaineth in me." Then He added, "And worlds without number have I created; and I also created them for mine own purpose. . . . The heavens, they are many, and they cannot be numbered unto man; but they are numbered unto me, for they are mine." (Moses 1:31, 33, 37.)

In some incomprehensible way, the Lord knows all of His creations intimately. He knows the heavens, the earth, and, more importantly, each individual on any one of the numberless earths. To leave no doubt in Moses' mind that numberless earths are not enough, the Lord continued, "As one earth shall pass away, and the heavens thereof even so shall another come; and there is no end to my works." (Moses 1:38.)

And then the Lord felt that Moses was ready to have his question answered. As Moses marveled and wondered—Why this earth? Why all the other earths? And why will there always be more?—the Savior gave him the answer: "For behold, this is my work and my glory—to bring to pass the immortality and eternal life of man." (Moses 1:39.)

The Savior is omnipotent. He is omniscient. With all this power and knowledge, what does He choose to do with His time? His whole purpose in being is to serve others by bringing to pass their immortality and eternal life. He has no other interest. His desire, which seems insatiable, is to lift others. He has an absolute, righteous need for an eternal expression, or outlet, for His infinite love.

This is a great chapter of scripture to me, not just because of the insights it gives us into the universe, but because of the insights it gives us into the love and unselfishness of the Lord.

The Savior is not looking toward retirement and relaxation. He is, and will be throughout all eternity, looking toward new opportunities to serve. We see this attitude perpetuated as He came to the earth to live as we live, only in much less comfort. While on this earth, He continued to think only of others. While here, He experienced all that we experience and more.

He "descended below [us] all" (D&C 122:8), but never do we see an account of agony about Himself. In one of the most painful times of His life, with His heart breaking for those who tormented Him, He said, "Father, forgive them; for they know not what they do." (Luke 23:34.) He was much more worried about the eternal consequences the acts of His enemies would have upon themselves than the temporary pain He was feeling as a result of their acts.

The Savior is omniscient and omnipotent, but never do we see Him use this knowledge and power to make His own life easier. He performed numerous miracles for others, but He would not perform a single miracle for His own benefit. Consider as an example the miracle of the bread and fish, recorded in Mark 6:34–44. He had taught the multitude long, and it was too late for them to obtain food. Therefore, He fed them by performing a miracle in order that they would not go hungry through the night.

On another occasion, Jesus turned water into wine. (See John 2:1–11.) This same Jehovah, at the time of Moses, sent manna from heaven for forty years because not to do so would mean the children of Israel would die in the wilderness. (See Exodus 16:31–35.)

On the other hand, when He Himself had fasted for forty days and forty nights, He refused the temptation of Satan to change the stones into bread for Himself. Satan chose the end of the fast, when the Savior's physical needs were the greatest, to tempt Him, saying, "If thou be the Son of God, command that these stones be made bread," to which the Savior answered, "Man shall not live by bread alone, but by every word that proceedeth out of the mouth of God." (Matthew 4:3–4.)

Could Jesus not have changed the stones into bread, or called for manna from heaven? Was He not justified in just a little miracle at the end of His forty-day fast? Elder McConkie has suggested that the reason He would not use His power in this way was because "Lucifer had made the providing of food for Jesus' hungry body a test of his divinity. 'If thou be the Son of God,' do this thing." (*The Mortal Messiah,* Book 1, *From Bethlehem to Calvary,* Salt Lake City: Deseret Book, p. 412.)

Elder Talmage suggests, however, that even if the question had been phrased in a way so as not to question His divinity, Jesus would not have performed this miracle for Himself. These powers were only to be used in the service of others. "The superior power that Jesus possessed had not been given to Him for personal gratification, but for service to others. He was to experience all the trials of mortality; another man, as hungry as He, could not provide for himself by a miracle; and though by miracle such a one might be fed, the miraculous supply would have to be given, not provided by himself. It was a necessary result of our Lord's dual nature, comprising the attributes of both God and man, that He should endure and suffer as a mortal while possessing at all times the ability to invoke the power of His own Godhood by which all bodily needs could be supplied or overcome. His reply to the tempter was sublime and positively final: 'It is written, Man shall not live by bread alone, but by every word that proceedeth out of the mouth of God.' " (*Jesus the Christ,* 1982 ed., pp. 121–22.)

The Lord could have performed the selfish miracle but would not. At the time of His betrayal and arrest, He said to those who wanted to fight: "Thinkest thou that I cannot now pray to my Father, and he shall presently give me more than twelve legions of angels? But how then shall the scriptures be fulfilled, that thus it must be?" (Matthew 26:53–54.) Again, the Lord could have used His powers to save Himself personal agony, but He would not. To have done so would have detracted from and even negated His mission.

Imagine the self-discipline and love Jesus has for us. He has all power and knowledge, but He has never taken unrighteous advantage of that power, and He never will, throughout all eternity, do so. Were He to do so, He would cease to be God.

If the Savior had chosen to squander His power or if He had had selfish desires, we might well assume He would have failed in His mission. He, as well as the Father, is bound by eternal, absolute truths. We have evidence of this in Alma's discourse on mercy and justice. Alma explains that the Lord is merciful, but there are limits to what He can do even if His heart wants to. "What, do ye suppose that mercy can rob justice? I say unto you, Nay; not one whit. If so, God would cease to be God." (Alma 42:25.)

Nephi, the son of Helaman, was an example of someone who had arrived at a godly state of total commitment to others. Because he had become Christlike and was totally consumed with the plight of others, he became one with God and Christ. The Savior was then able to give him the ultimate trust: "Blessed art thou, Nephi, for those things which thou hast done; for I have beheld how thou hast with unwearyingness declared the word, which I have given unto thee, unto this people. And thou hast not feared them, and hast not sought thine own life, but hast sought my will, and to keep my commandments. And now, because thou hast done this with such unwearyingness, behold, I will bless thee forever; and I will make thee mighty in word and in deed, in faith and in works; yea, even that all things shall be done unto thee according to thy word, for thou shalt not ask that which is contrary to my will." (Helaman 10:4–5.)

Grasping this eternal concept helps us understand Doctrine and Covenants 121:36, where we read that "the rights of the priesthood are inseparably connected with the powers of heaven, and that the powers of heaven cannot be controlled nor handled only upon the principles of righteousness." The only way we can increase our strength is to give away that which we receive.

We have many modern-day examples of unselfishness. I remember an interview of President Spencer W. Kimball by a member of the media. President and Sister Kimball lived in a modest home in an average neighborhood. The interviewer asked, "Now that you are the President of the Church, why don't you move into a more comfortable home?" President Kimball looked genuinely puzzled and replied, "What on earth would be gained by that?" It had never occurred to him that his standard of living should be changed as a result of his new status.

In a world going crazy with people roaming to and fro trying to find themselves, the Lord's counsel rings clearly in the ears of those who will listen: "Whosoever will save his life shall lose it: and whosoever will lose his life for my sake shall find it." (Matthew 16:25.)

Unselfishness marked every action of the Savior. Personal pleasures and comfort all came last, if at all. He spent his ministry serving others. As great as was His suffering on the cross and in Gethsemane, I am touched by His day-to-day service prior to that appointed hour. As He explained to one disciple who wanted to join Him, "Foxes have holes, and birds of the air have nests; but the Son of man hath not where to lay his head." (Luke 9:58.)

Prior to His birth, during His earthly life, and into the eternal future, the Savior has continued to give and give and give. Why? He has infinite love for us, individually and collectively. To feel His love personally is one of life's greatest blessings. To feel that same love for Him is another blessing. However, to feel that love for all mankind is the ultimate goal. Until we have pure love for all men, our love of the Savior is incomplete. We gain this love in increments that are directly related to living our lives in the service of others.

Many people in the world, including some Latter-day Saints, spend their whole lives looking for that which will permanently satisfy some infinite cravings of the soul. Some turn to power; others to sex, drugs, money, travel, and an infinite smorgasbord served up by the world. Once they have subdued one goal, they soon find their craving has not been eliminated, and they charge off into another direction.

That seemingly insatiable craving is inborn into all spirit children of our Father in Heaven. It can be fulfilled and satisfied only when we lose ourselves in the service of others. By so doing, we begin to feel the Savior's love for us, the love of our fellowman for us, and a Christlike love for the Savior and all God's children. That love sometimes feels as if it is going to consume us, but instead it purifies, sanctifies, and satisfies.

The joy of feeling Christlike love for others is indescribable and delicious to the taste. Can we comprehend such love? While on this earth, perhaps we can only obtain a finite understanding, but as we reach out in pure love to serve others, we do get a glimpse into infinite love. Service is not the price we pay to earn the celestial kingdom. Service is the very fiber of which the celestial kingdom is made.

As we remain true to our covenants and go through the trials and sorrows of this life with our hearts turned toward the Lord, something begins to happen to our nature. Through the gift of God, by the power of the Holy Spirit, a metamorphosis takes place, which we have referred to as purification and sanctification. As this evolves, our thoughts and actions are turned from our own problems to feeling compassion and empathy for others. This is demonstrated by spontaneous acts of Christian service.

As we lose our lives in serving others, each of us can find our life. We can discover a great truth: True happiness can be found only when we are lifting others. Our whole disposition is turned to doing good, and we have no disposition to do evil. We have arrived on the second plateau.

Third Plateau

Spiritual
Graduate
School

11

Mysteries, Miracles, and Signs

What more could we ask for than to reach the second plateau, sanctification? Nothing, really, because once we have reached that plateau, we have accomplished what we were sent to earth to do. We have accepted the gospel, placed our faith in the atonement of Jesus Christ, repented, and become very much like Him. With this oneness, our life is filled with good deeds, all done for the right reason because it has become our disposition to do so. Nevertheless, the Lord continues to bless us with what we need in our eternal progression. To those who sanctify themselves, a third plateau emerges.

I have entitled the third plateau "spiritual graduate school." There are blessings available to those who have become substantially purified or sanctified, blessings that are reserved for the pure in heart. From the moment we become converted, we receive personal revelation through the Holy Ghost. This is what takes us to the testimony plateau. Revelation increases as we travel the difficult trail of the sanctification process. At some point on that spectrum, another vista opens to us. The timing is impossible to pinpoint, for it depends on our circumstances, need, and righteousness. This spiritual graduate school is a continuum, but some aspects of the training definitely come when we prove ourselves by our endurance.

Modern-day revelation tells us: "Whatever principle of intelligence we attain unto in this life, it will rise with us in the resurrection. And if a person gains more knowledge and intelligence in this life through his diligence and obedience than another, he will have so much the advantage in the world to come. There is a law, irrevocably decreed in heaven before the foundations of this world, upon which all blessings are predicated—and when we obtain any blessing from God, it is by obedience to that law upon which it is predicated." (D&C 130:18–21.)

As this scripture points out, the receipt of a blessing depends upon obedience to the law upon which it is predicated. The blessing of spiritual graduate school comes as a person becomes purified and sanctified. Sometimes this advanced information is referred to as mysteries of the kingdom. In the first verse in the Book of Mormon, we are introduced to this reality: "I, Nephi, having been born of goodly parents, therefore I was taught somewhat in all the learning of my father; and having seen many afflictions in the course of my days, nevertheless, having been highly favored of the Lord in all my days; yea, having had a great knowledge of the goodness and the mysteries of God, therefore I make a record of my proceedings in my days." (1 Nephi 1:1.)

Of special note relative to the theme of this book is that Nephi refers to all three plateaus in this verse: testimony, sanctification (through his afflictions), and spiritual graduate school (knowledge of the mysteries of God). Many other scriptures invite us to learn these truths. Here are just a few:

"It is given unto you [Jesus' disciples] to know the mysteries of the kingdom of heaven, but to them [those who are not spiritually attuned] it is not given." (Matthew 13:11.)

"Let a man so account of us, as of the ministers of Christ, and stewards of the mysteries of God." (1 Corinthians 4:1.)

"And it came to pass that I, Nephi, being exceedingly young, nevertheless being large in stature, and also having great desires to know of the mysteries of God, wherefore, I did cry unto the Lord; and behold he did visit me, and did soften my heart that I did believe all the words which had been spoken by my father; wherefore, I did not rebel against him like unto my brothers."(1 Nephi 2:16.)

"For he that diligently seeketh shall find; and the mysteries of God shall be unfolded unto them, by the power of the Holy Ghost, as well in these times as in times of old, and as well in times of old as in times to come; wherefore, the course of the Lord is one eternal round." (1 Nephi 10:19.)

"Yea, he that repenteth and exerciseth faith, and bringeth forth good works, and prayeth continually without ceasing—unto such it is given to know the mysteries of God; yea, unto such it shall be given to reveal things which never have been revealed; yea, and it shall be given unto such to bring thousands of souls to repentance, even as it has been given unto us to bring these our brethren to repentance." (Alma 26:22.)

"If thou shalt ask, thou shalt receive revelation upon revelation, knowledge upon knowledge, that thou mayest know the mysteries and peaceable things—that which bringeth joy, that which bringeth life eternal." (D&C 42:61.)

"Seek not for riches but for wisdom, and behold, the mysteries of God shall be unfolded unto you, and then shall you be made rich. Behold, he that hath eternal life is rich." (D&C 6:7.)

"And to them [the righteous] will I reveal all mysteries, yea, all the hidden mysteries of my kingdom from days of old, and for ages to come, will I make known unto them the good pleasure of my will concerning all things pertaining to my kingdom." (D&C 76:7.)

"The power and authority of the higher, or Melchizedek Priesthood, is to hold the keys of all the spiritual blessings of the church—to have the privilege of receiving the mysteries of the kingdom of heaven, to have the heavens opened unto them, to commune with the general assembly and church of the Firstborn, and to enjoy the communion and presence of God the Father, and Jesus the mediator of the new covenant." (D&C 107:18–19.)

As these scriptures demonstrate, mysteries are revealed to those who obey the law upon which the blessing is predicated.

We also learn that signs follow those who believe. The appropriate purpose of signs is given in section 63 of the Doctrine and Covenants: "Verily, I say unto you, there are those among you who seek signs, and there have been such even from the beginning; but, behold, faith cometh not by signs, but signs follow those that believe." (D&C 63:8–9.)

From this we learn there is nothing inherently evil in signs; in fact, they are a natural consequence of righteousness. They are gifts from God to those who purify themselves before Him. However, we are not to seek after them for physical proof of what the Spirit has revealed to us. Once we have accepted and believed what the Spirit tells us, signs follow.

President Spencer W. Kimball said, "Signs will *follow* them that believe. He makes no promise that signs will create belief nor save nor exalt. Signs are the product of faith. They are born in the soil of unwavering sureness. They will be prevalent in the Church in about the same degree to which the people have true faith." (*Teachings of Spencer W. Kimball,* p. 500.)

President Brigham Young said: "Miracles, or these extraordinary manifestations of the power of God, are not for the unbeliever; they are to console the Saints, and to strengthen and confirm the faith of those who love, fear, and serve God, and not for outsiders." (*Discourses of Brigham Young,* Salt Lake City: Deseret Book, 1954, p. 341.)

From Elder James E. Talmage we learn: "Miracles are not primarily intended, surely they are not needed, to prove the power of God; the simpler occurrences, the more ordinary works of creation do that. But unto the heart already softened and purified by the testimony of the truth, to the mind enlightened through the Spirit's power and conscious of obedient service in the requirements of the

Gospel, the voice of miracles comes with cheering tidings, with fresh and more abundant evidences of the magnanimity of an all merciful God." (*Articles of Faith,* 1984 ed., p. 199.)

Elder Bruce R. McConkie put it this way: "Miracles are part of the gospel. Signs follow those that believe. Where the doctrines of salvation are taught in purity and perfection, where there are believing souls who accept these truths and make them a part of their lives, and where devout souls accept Jesus as their Lord and serve him to the best of their ability, there will always be miracles. Such ever attend the preaching of the gospel to receptive and conforming people. Miracles stand as a sign and a witness of the truth and divinity of the Lord's work. Where there are miracles, there is the gospel, the Church, the kingdom, and the hope of salvation. Where there are no signs and miracles, none of these desired blessings will be found." (*The Mortal Messiah* 2:10.)

Elder McConkie also wrote: *"Signs flow from faith.* They may incidentally have the effect of strengthening the faith of those who are already spiritually inclined, but *their chief purpose is not to convert people to the truth, but to reward and bless those already converted.* . . . To seek the gifts of the Spirit through faith, humility, and devotion to righteousness is not to be confused with sign-seeking. The saints are commanded to 'covet earnestly the best gifts.' (1 Cor. 12:31.) But implicit in this exhortation is the presumption that those so seeking will do so in the way the Lord has ordained." (*Mormon Doctrine,* pp. 713, 715.)

Many of us have heard the counsel, "Don't get into the mysteries." Elder McConkie sheds light on this seeming inconsistency: "There is . . . a restricted and limited usage of the expression *mysteries;* it is more of a colloquial than a scriptural usage, and it has reference to that body of teachings in the speculative field, those things which the Lord has not revealed in plainness in this day. It is to these things that reference is made when the elders are counseled to leave the mysteries alone.

" 'Oh, ye elders of Israel, hearken to my voice,' the Prophet said, 'and when you are sent into the world to preach, tell those things you are sent to tell; preach and cry aloud, "Repent ye, for the kingdom of heaven is at hand; repent and believe the gospel." Declare the first principles, and let mysteries alone, lest ye be overthrown. Never meddle with the visions of beasts and subjects you do not understand.' (*Teachings,* p. 292.)" (Ibid., p. 524.)

Mysteries are elusive because as soon as one understands a concept, it is no longer a mystery. The gospel itself is a mystery to the world at large. The fact that God the Father has a body of flesh and bones is a mystery to most of mankind. Latter-day Saints take for granted the wealth of mysteries that have been revealed in this last dispensation. Mysteries of general knowledge are received on the first and second plateaus. The mysteries on the third plateau are reserved for those who have obtained a certain amount of purification.

Let me illustrate this by quoting and elaborating on my favorite scriptures on this subject. You are familiar with Lehi's vision of the tree of life and that he explained this vision to his family. This was Nephi's reaction: "And it came to pass after I, Nephi, having heard all the words of my father, concerning the things which he saw in a vision, and also the things which he spake by the power of the Holy Ghost. . . . I, Nephi, was desirous also that I might see, and hear, and know of these things, by the power of the Holy Ghost, which is the gift of God unto all those who diligently seek him." (1 Nephi 10:17.)

Notice that Nephi did not pray, "Heavenly Father, bless me that I might know that what my father saw was true." He said he was desirous to have the same vision.

Nephi continued: "For it came to pass after I had desired to know the things that my father had seen, and believing that the Lord was able to make them known unto me, as I sat pondering in mine heart I was caught away in the Spirit of the Lord, yea, into an exceedingly high mountain, which I never had before seen, and upon which I never had before set my foot." (1 Nephi 11:1.)

Then Nephi went on to recount that he saw the things his father had seen. He was not content to live by the testimony of his father. He wanted to experience these things and know them for himself. This was not idle curiosity or selfishness. He was not seeking a sign. It was a righteous desire. He already had an unshakable testimony, and all evidence suggests he had experienced the mighty change of heart. The Lord said to him, "Blessed art thou, Nephi, because thou believest in the Son of the most high God; wherefore, thou shalt behold the things which thou hast desired." (1 Nephi 11:6.)

Nephi was shown the same vision as his father. It was in this context that he wrote: "He that diligently seeketh shall find; and the mysteries of God shall be unfolded unto them, by the power of the Holy Ghost, as well in these times as in times of old, and as well in times of old as in times to come; wherefore, the course of the Lord is one eternal round." (1 Nephi 10:19.)

In the Doctrine and Covenants we are told: "If your

eye be single to my glory, your whole bodies shall be filled with light, and there shall be no darkness in you; and that body which is filled with light comprehendeth all things. Therefore, sanctify yourselves that your minds become single to God, and the days will come that you shall see him; for he will unveil his face unto you, and it shall be in his own time, and in his own way, and according to his own will." (D&C 88:67–68.)

This scripture illustrates my point that some spiritual insights are reserved for those who have sanctified and purified themselves, insights that would not be available to those who have not paid the price.

When section 76 of the Doctrine and Covenants is mentioned, most of us think of the three degrees of glory. This is another example of a mystery not understood by the world in general. Also included in this section is the majestic vision of the Father and His Son. Joseph Smith recorded: "We beheld the glory of the Son, on the right hand of the Father, and received of his fulness; and saw the holy angels, and them who are sanctified before his throne, worshiping God, and the Lamb, who worship him forever and ever. And now, after the many testimonies which have been given of him, this is the testimony, last of all, which we give of him: That he lives! For we saw him, even on the right hand of God; and we heard the voice bearing record that he is the Only Begotten of the Father—that by him, and through him, and of him, the worlds are and were created, and the inhabitants thereof are begotten sons and daughters unto God." (D&C 76:20–24.)

The last verses of section 76 are some of the greatest scriptural beckonings to the third plateau in holy writ. Unfortunately, in many of our gospel discussions we never reach the end of that section. One reason may be that too often we get into a debate as to whether or not one can progress from one degree of glory to the other. We also tend to think up every hypothetical situation possible and argue over to which degree of glory each person would be assigned. In other words, we delve into the speculative mysteries—and while thus engaged, we don't catch the vision of supernal truth available to us if we are willing to pay the price.

After disclosing the vision of the Father and the Son, the three degrees of glory, and many other beautiful truths that had previously been mysteries to all mankind, Joseph Smith concluded the revelation as follows: "Great and marvelous are the works of the Lord, and the mysteries of his kingdom which he showed unto us, which surpass all understanding in glory, and in might, and in dominion; which he commanded us we should not write while we were yet in the Spirit, and are not lawful for man to utter." (D&C 76:114–15.)

The Prophet almost seems to be teasing us by saying, in effect, "If you think what we've written is exciting, you should have seen what else we saw, but we can't tell you." However, in reading the next verses we find the commandment wasn't necessary, because words could not describe it: "Neither is man capable to make them known, for they are only to be seen and understood by the power of the Holy Spirit, which God bestows on those who love him, and purify themselves before him; to whom he grants this privilege of seeing and knowing for themselves; that through the power and manifestation of the Spirit, while in the flesh, they may be able to bear his presence in the world of glory." (D&C 76:116–18.)

Note the condition upon which the blessing is predicated: purification, the second plateau.

A similar invitation is made in section 93: "Verily, thus saith the Lord: It shall come to pass that every soul who forsaketh his sins and cometh unto me, and calleth on my name, and obeyeth my voice, and keepeth my commandments, shall see my face and know that I am." (D&C 93:1.)

Hence, some things that are available to those who "purify themselves before him" are not disclosed to the general membership of the Church, let alone the world. These things I am classifying as spiritual graduate school.

Since God is no respecter of persons, all who purify and sanctify their lives (the second plateau) have access to learning the mysteries of the kingdom. As Elder McConkie put it: "Personal revelation is not limited to gaining a testimony and knowing thereby that Jesus, through whom the gospel came, is Lord of all, nor is it limited to receiving guidance in our personal and family affairs—although these are the most common examples of revelation among the Lord's people. In truth and in verity, there is no limit to the revelations each member of the Church may receive. It is within the power of every person who has received the gift of the Holy Ghost to see visions, entertain angels, learn the deep and hidden mysteries of the kingdom." (*A New Witness for the Articles of Faith*, Salt Lake City: Deseret Book, 1985, pp. 489–90.)

In the Doctrine and Covenants we are told that the key to the third plateau is the Melchizedek Priesthood: "This greater priesthood administereth the gospel and holdeth the key of the mysteries of the kingdom, even the key of the knowledge of God. Therefore, in the ordinances thereof, the power of godliness is manifest. And without the ordinances thereof, and the authority of the priesthood, the power of godliness is not manifest unto men in the flesh; for without this no man can see the face of God, even the Father, and live." (D&C 84:19–22.)

Commenting on section 84, Joseph Fielding Smith said: "It is impossible for men to obtain the knowledge of the mysteries of the kingdom or the knowledge of God, without the authority of the Priesthood. Secular learning, the study of the sciences, arts and history, will not reveal these vital truths to men. It is the Holy Priesthood that unlocks the door to heaven and reveals to man the mysteries of the Kingdom of God. It is this Divine Authority which makes known the knowledge of God! Is there any wonder that the world today is groping in gross darkness concerning God and the things of his kingdom? We should also remember that these great truths are not made known even to members of the Church unless they place their lives in harmony with the law on which these blessings are predicated." (*Church History and Modern Revelation*, Salt Lake City: Deseret Book, 1953, 1:338.)

It should go without saying that the blessings are available to male and female alike. We sometimes confuse the privilege of *holding* the priesthood with the *blessings* of the priesthood. Blessings of the priesthood are far greater than those concerned with holding the priesthood. The ordinances and covenants of the priesthood and remaining true to them are what bring forth the blessings.

On this subject President Smith said: "It ought to make every man among us who holds the priesthood rejoice to think that we have that great authority by which *we may know God.* Not only the men holding the priesthood know that great truth, but because of that priesthood and the *ordinances thereof,* every member of the Church, men and women alike, may know God." (*Doctrines of Salvation,* Salt Lake City: Bookcraft, vol. 3, 1956, pp. 142–43.)

12

Third Plateau
Experiences of Today

Blessings of the third plateau are available to all and are present in the Church today. According to the Book of Mormon, those things will always be with the Church as long as there are righteous people:

"Wherefore, my beloved brethren, have miracles ceased because Christ hath ascended into heaven, and hath sat down on the right hand of God, to claim of the Father his rights of mercy which he hath upon the children of men? For he hath answered the ends of the law, and he claimeth all those who have faith in him; and they who have faith in him will cleave unto every good thing; wherefore he advocateth the cause of the children of men; and he dwelleth eternally in the heavens.

"And because he hath done this, my beloved brethren, have miracles ceased? Behold I say unto you, Nay; neither have angels ceased to minister unto the children of men. For behold, they are subject unto him, to minister according to the word of his command, showing themselves unto them of strong faith and a firm mind in every form of godliness. And the office of their ministry is to call men unto repentance, and to fulfil and to do the work of the covenants of the Father, which he hath made unto the children of men, to prepare the way among the children of men, by declaring the word of Christ unto the chosen vessels of the Lord, that they may bear testimony of him. . . .

"And now, my beloved brethren, if this be the case that these things are true which I have spoken unto you, and God will show unto you, with power and great glory at the last day, that they are true, and if they are true has the day of miracles ceased? Or have angels ceased to appear unto the children of men? Or has he withheld the power of the Holy Ghost from them? Or will he, so long as time shall last, or the earth shall stand, or there shall be one man upon the face thereof to be saved? Behold I say unto you, Nay; for it is by faith that miracles are wrought; and it is by faith that angels appear and minister unto men; wherefore, if these things have ceased wo be unto the children of men, for it is because of unbelief, and all is vain." (Moroni 7:27–31, 35–37.)

Modern-day prophets have testified to that reality. Elder Boyd K. Packer has said: "We who have been called to lead the Church are ordinary men and women with ordinary capacities struggling to administer a church which grows at such a pace as to astound even those who watch it closely. Some are disposed to find fault with us; surely that is easy for them to do. But they do not examine us more searchingly than we examine ourselves. A call to lead is not an exemption from the challenges of life. We seek for inspiration in the same way that you do, and we must obey the same laws which apply to every member of the Church.

"We are sorry for our inadequacies, sorry we are not better than we are. We can feel, as you can see, the effect of the aging process as it imposes limitations upon His leaders before your very eyes.

"But this we know. There are councils and counselors and quorums to counterbalance the foibles and frailties of man. The Lord organized His church to provide for mortal men to work as mortal men, and yet He assured that the spirit of revelation would guide in all that we do in His name.

"And in the end, what is given comes because the Lord has spoken it, 'whether by [His] own voice or by the voice of [His] servants, it is the same.' (D&C 1:38.) We know His voice when He speaks.

"Revelation continues with us today. The promptings of the Spirit, the dreams, the visions and the visitations, and the ministering of angels all are with us now. And the still, small voice of the Holy Ghost 'is a lamp unto [our] feet, and a light unto [our] path.' (Psalm 119:105.)" (*Ensign,* November 1989, p. 16.)

To this I add the sacred testimony and experience of Elder David B. Haight, which he shared in general conference:

"Six months ago at the April general conference, I was excused from speaking as I was convalescing from a serious operation. My life has been spared, and I now have the pleasant opportunity of acknowledging the blessings, comfort, and ready aid of my Brethren in the First Presidency and Quorum of the Twelve, and other wonderful associates and friends to whom I owe so much and who surrounded my dear wife, Ruby, and my family with their time, attention, and prayers. . . .

"The evening of my health crisis, I knew something very serious had happened to me. Events happened so swiftly—the pain striking with such intensity, my dear Ruby phoning the doctor and our family, and I on my knees leaning over the bathtub for support and some comfort and hoped relief from the pain. I was pleading to my Heavenly Father to spare my life a while longer to give me a little more time to do His work, if it was His will.

"While still praying, I began to lose consciousness. The siren of the paramedic truck was the last that I remembered before unconsciousness overtook me, which would last for the next several days.

"The terrible pain and commotion of people ceased. I was now in a calm, peaceful setting; all was serene and quiet. I was conscious of two persons in the distance on a hillside, one standing on a higher level than the other. Detailed features were not discernible. The person on the higher level was pointing to something I could not see.

"I heard no voices but was conscious of being in a holy presence and atmosphere. During the hours and days that followed, there was impressed again and again upon my mind the eternal mission and exalted position of the Son of Man.

"I witness to you that He is Jesus the Christ, the Son of God, Savior to all, Redeemer of all mankind, Bestower of infinite love, mercy, and forgiveness, the Light and Life of the world. I knew this truth before—I had never doubted nor wondered. But now I knew, because of the impressions of the Spirit upon my heart and soul, these divine truths in a most unusual way.

"I was shown a panoramic view of His earthly ministry: His baptism, His teaching, His healing the sick and lame, the mock trial, His crucifixion, His resurrection and ascension. There followed scenes of His earthly ministry to my mind in impressive detail, confirming scriptural eyewitness accounts. I was being taught, and the eyes of my understanding were opened by the Holy Spirit of God so as to behold many things. . . .

"During those days of unconsciousness I was given, by the gift and power of the Holy Ghost, a more perfect knowledge of His mission. I was also given a more complete understanding of what it means to exercise, in His name, the authority to unlock the mysteries of the kingdom of heaven for the salvation of all who are faithful. My soul was taught over and over again. . . .

"I cannot begin to convey to you the deep impact that these scenes have confirmed upon my soul. . . . I testify to all of you that our Heavenly Father does answer our righteous pleadings. The added knowledge which has come to me has made a great impact upon my life. The gift of the Holy Ghost is a priceless possession and opens the door to our ongoing knowledge of God and eternal joy. Of this I bear witness, in the holy name of Jesus Christ, amen." (*Ensign,* November 1989, pp. 59–61.)

While these testimonies are from two of the Lord's special witnesses, I reemphasize that God is no respecter of persons, and that these blessings come as a result of purity, not position.

As a general rule, this type of revelation is reserved

for the pure in heart. It comes after a trial of faith. Faith precedes the miracle. Why is it reserved for those who have proven themselves? If we do not learn how to recognize the truth of unseen things, we will not be able to discern the source of physical manifestations. For every spiritual gift or manifestation from the Lord, Satan has a counterfeit.

Sometimes people struggling with a testimony (especially transgressors who are losing the testimony they once had) will pray for manifestations of the third plateau. Satan hears and obliges them. Inasmuch as these persons have lost the discernment of the Spirit—or have not matured in the gospel enough to have ever acquired it—they accept the manifestation as having come from the Lord. Satan then leads them carefully away from the Church and often into open rebellion against it.

As Elder Talmage put it: "Specified gifts of the Spirit are to follow the believer as signs of divine acknowledgment. The possession of such gifts may be taken therefore as essential features of the Church of Jesus Christ. Nevertheless, we are not justified in regarding the evidence of miracles as proof of authority from heaven; on the other hand, the scriptures aver that spiritual powers of the baser sort have wrought miracles, and will continue so to do, to the deceiving of many who lack discernment. . . . John the Revelator saw in vision a wicked power working miracles, and thereby deceiving many, doing great wonders, even bringing fire from heaven. Again, he saw unclean spirits, whom he knew to be 'the spirits of devils, working miracles.' " (*Articles of Faith*, 1984 ed., p. 209.)

President Joseph F. Smith said: "The gifts of the Spirit and the powers of the holy Priesthood are of God, they are given for the blessing of the people, for their encouragement, and for the strengthening of their faith. This Satan knows full well, therefore he seeks by imitation-miracles to blind and deceive the children of God. Remember what the magicians of Egypt accomplished in their efforts to deceive Pharaoh as to the divinity of the mission of Moses and Aaron. John the Revelator saw in vision the miracle-working power of the evil one. Note his words. 'And I beheld another beast coming up out of the earth; . . . and he doeth great wonders, so that he maketh fire come down from heaven on the earth in the sight of men. And deceiveth them that dwell on the earth, by the means of those miracles,' etc. (Rev. 13:11–14.) Further, John saw three unclean spirits whom he describes as 'the spirits of devils, working miracles.' (Rev. 16:13–14.)" (*Gospel Doctrine*, p. 376.)

With these truths in mind, it is easier to understand why I suggest the chronology of the spiritual plateaus: testimony, sanctification, and spiritual graduate school. The revelations of which we have been speaking come subsequent to sanctification in order that they will not be mocked by one not ready to receive them, or imitated by the evil one. Satan's counterfeit cannot fool a person who, through faithfulness, has acquired the ability to discern good from evil. That person has already learned to discern the truth of things unseen and is now qualified to discern the truth and source of things seen.

These things are not talked of much by those who have experienced them, because they are personal and sacred. Alma said: "It is given unto many to know the mysteries of God; nevertheless they are laid under a strict command that they shall not impart only according to the portion of his word which he doth grant unto the children of men, according to the heed and diligence which they give unto him. And therefore, he that will harden his heart, the same receiveth the lesser portion of the word; and he that will not harden his heart, to him is given the greater portion of the word, until it is given unto him to know the mysteries of God until he know them in full." (Alma 12:9–10.)

Elder Widtsoe said: "Divine manifestations for individual comfort may be received by every worthy member of the Church. In that respect all faithful members of the Church are equal. Such manifestations most commonly guide the recipients to the solution of personal problems; though, frequently, they also open the mind to a clearer comprehension of the Lord's vast plan of salvation. They are cherished possessions, and should be so valued by those who receive them. In their very nature, they are sacred and should be so treated." (*Evidences and Reconciliations*, pp. 98–99.)

When asked, inappropriately, "Have you ever had any spectacular spiritual experiences from beyond the veil?," someone once wisely answered, "Nothing to speak of."

While we hold such experiences sacred, those who have received counterfeit manifestations from the evil one often shout them from the rooftops and publish them in newspapers. It is horrifying to see how misled some individuals can become. Some who break sacred moral commandments and even commit violent crimes will use as a justification, "I received a revelation." As members of Christ's church, we must always remember that beautiful, spiritual things have a dark and opposite side. Satan is willing and able to produce his own miracles. He does not hold them sacred.

Elder Packer has said, "All inspiration does not come from God. (See D&C 46:7.) The evil one has the power to tap into those channels of revelation and send conflicting signals which can mislead and confuse us. There are promptings from evil sources which are so carefully counterfeited as to deceive even the very elect. (See Matthew 24:24.) Nevertheless, we can learn to discern these spirits. Even with every member having the right to revelation, the Church can be maintained as a house of order." (*Ensign,* November 1989, p. 14.)

Moses is an example of a person who had a physical witness of the Savior, followed by a physical visit from Satan. At the time both were spirits. Regarding Moses' experience, we read: "[Moses] saw God face to face, and he talked with him, and the glory of God was upon Moses; therefore Moses could endure his presence. And God spake unto Moses, saying: Behold, I am the Lord God Almighty, and Endless is my name; for I am without beginning of days or end of years; and is not this endless?" (Moses 1:2–3.)

The Lord then showed Moses the world in its completeness: "And it came to pass that Moses looked, and beheld the world upon which he was created; and Moses beheld the world and the ends thereof, and all the children of men which are, and which were created; of the same he greatly marveled and wondered." (Moses 1:8.)

In other words, the Lord revealed some mysteries to Moses. Then, we read, "The presence of God withdrew from Moses, that his glory was not upon Moses; and Moses was left unto himself. And as he was left unto himself, he fell unto the earth. And it came to pass that it was for the space of many hours before Moses did again receive his natural strength like unto man; and he said unto himself: Now, for this cause I know that man is nothing, which thing I never had supposed. But now mine own eyes have beheld God; but not my natural, but my spiritual eyes, for my natural eyes could not have beheld; for I should have withered and died in his presence; but his glory was upon me; and I beheld his face, for I was transfigured before him." (Moses 1:9–11.)

Immediately thereafter, Satan appeared to Moses and tempted him, saying, "Moses, son of man, worship me." (Moses 1:12.)

Moses had two reasons for seeing through Satan. First, he had just seen the Lord and could compare the two visits. He could see a difference in the glory. He told Satan, "I could not look upon God, except his glory should come upon me, and I were transfigured before him. But I can look upon thee in the natural man. Is it not so, surely?" (Moses 1:14.)

The second reason was that by the discernment of the Spirit, Moses could tell that this spectacular manifestation was not of God: "Blessed be the name of my God, for his Spirit hath not altogether withdrawn from me, or else where is thy glory, for it is darkness unto me? And I can judge between thee and God; for God said unto me: Worship God, for him only shalt thou serve. Get thee hence, Satan; deceive me not; for God said unto me: Thou art after the similitude of mine Only Begotten. And he also gave me commandments when he called unto me out of the burning bush, saying: Call upon God in the name of mine Only Begotten, and worship me. And again Moses said: I will not cease to call upon God, I have other things to inquire of him: *for his glory has been upon me, wherefore I can judge between him and thee.* Depart hence, Satan." (Moses 1:15–18; italics added.)

Moses had reached a level of sanctification whereby he could discern the source of a physical manifestation. He commanded Satan to leave, at which Satan became very angry and, showing his true ugliness, had a temper tantrum: "Now Satan began to tremble, and the earth shook; and Moses received strength, and called upon God, saying: In the name of the Only Begotten, depart hence, Satan. And it came to pass that Satan cried with a loud voice, with weeping, and wailing, and gnashing of teeth; and he departed hence, even from the presence of Moses, that he beheld him not." (Moses 1:21–22.)

Again, we see the very real power of Satan and his ability to do miraculous things. The earth shook, but he was dismissed by the higher power. Should Satan and his angels appear to someone of less spiritual maturity than Moses and demonstrate their powers, it is possible that that person could be misled. Consequently, there is a reason for the chronology of the plateaus.

13

The Still
Small Voice

We have reviewed scriptures relative to the mysteries of the kingdom. I have also pointed out through the scriptures that miracles have not ceased nor have visions, dreams, and visitations of angels. My objective has been to awaken us to our individual spiritual potential. I would now like to bring these more "spectacular" revelations into perspective. I will have done a great injustice to the seeker of truth if anyone has been led to the conclusion that all "spiritual graduate school" is taught by visions, dreams, and visitations. In fact, quite the opposite is true. Mysteries of the kingdom are taught for the most part by the Spirit of the Holy Ghost as we ponder the scriptures for answers to our soul's questions.

We may have read the Book of Mormon many times, but between readings we experience life and the sanctification that accompanies a true Saint. Because of our experiences, the current reading can trigger a depth of understanding not previously grasped. We constantly "discover" new scriptures in the same book. In the process, the Holy Ghost gives customized revelation to each individual to suit his or her level of spiritual development. Sometimes we search out people with whom to share our new insight. Sometimes the individual gives us a look that implies, "Did you just discover that?" Other individuals can't comprehend what we are talking about because they are not yet ready. Gradually we gain the wisdom to rely on the Spirit to let us know what should and what should not be shared and with whom we should or should not share.

The still small voice is the vehicle most commonly used for educating us on the mysteries of the kingdom, just as it is the vehicle most commonly used for relaying the truthfulness of the gospel to investigators. The experience we gain in listening to this voice in gaining our testimonies and going through the sanctification helps develop the skill necessary for spiritual graduate school.

Therefore, the fact that a person has not received a vision or visitation does not mean "spiritual graduate school" has not yet begun. One plateau leads to another. There are no clear distinctions in leaving one and entering another. We receive line upon line, precept upon precept. In the Book of Mormon we read: "Now, my beloved brethren, after ye have gotten into this strait and narrow path, I would ask if all is done? Behold, I say unto you, Nay; for ye have not come thus far save it were by the word of Christ with unshaken faith in him, relying wholly upon the merits of him who is mighty to save. Wherefore, ye must press forward with a steadfastness in Christ, having a perfect brightness of hope, and a love of God and of all men. Wherefore, if ye shall press forward, feasting upon the word of Christ, and endure to the end, behold, thus saith the Father: Ye shall have eternal life." (2 Nephi 31:19–20.)

And in the Doctrine and Covenants: "Behold, ye are little children and ye cannot bear all things now; ye must grow in grace and in the knowledge of the truth. Fear not, little children, for you are mine, and I have overcome the world, and you are of them that my Father hath given me; and none of them that my Father hath given me shall be lost. And the Father and I are one. I am in the Father and the Father in me; and inasmuch as ye have received me, ye are in me and I in you. Wherefore, I am in your midst, and I am the good shepherd, and the stone of Israel. He that buildeth upon this rock shall never fail. And the day cometh that you shall hear my voice and see me, and know that I am." (D&C 50:40–45.)

We know there are many gifts of the Spirit. The Doctrine and Covenants delineates them very well in section 46. I would like to make several points relating to the gifts that are relevant to our spiritual progress through the plateaus. In verse 7, we are told to beware of being seduced by evil spirits: "Ye are commanded in all things to ask of God, who giveth liberally; and that which the Spirit testifies unto you even so I would that ye should do in all holiness of heart, walking uprightly before me, considering the end of your salvation, doing all things with prayer and thanksgiving, that ye may not be seduced by evil spirits, or doctrines of devils, or the commandments of men; for some are of men, and others of devils."

In verse 8, we are told, "Seek ye earnestly the best gifts, always remembering for what they are given."

Then in verses 9 and 10, we are told why the gifts are given: "They are given for the benefit of those who love me and keep all my commandments, and him that seeketh so to do; that all may be benefited that seek or that ask of me, that ask and not for a sign that they may consume it upon their lusts. And again, verily I say unto you, I would that ye should always remember, and always retain in your minds what those gifts are, that are given unto the church."

These gifts are to keep us moving toward exaltation and to help build our testimonies, love, sanctification, and, I would suggest, spiritual schooling. They are for the benefit of the membership of the Church individually and collectively. However, although many gifts are available, we are instructed that not everyone has every gift:

"For all have not every gift given unto them; for there are many gifts, and to every man is given a gift by the Spirit of God. To some is given one, and to some is given another, that all may be profited thereby.

"To some it is given by the Holy Ghost to know that Jesus Christ is the Son of God, and that he was crucified for the sins of the world. To others it is given to believe on their words, that they also might have eternal life if they continue faithful. And again, to some it is given by the Holy Ghost to know the differences of administration, as it will be pleasing unto the same Lord, according as the Lord will, suiting his mercies according to the conditions of the children of men. And again, it is given by the Holy Ghost to some to know the diversities of operations, whether they be of God, that the manifestations of the Spirit may be given to every man to profit withal.

"And again, verily I say unto you, to some is given, by the Spirit of God, the word of wisdom. To another is given the word of knowledge, that all may be taught to be wise, and to have knowledge.

"And again, to some it is given to have faith to be healed; and to others it is given to have faith to heal.

"And again, to some is given the working of miracles; and to others it is given to prophesy; and to others the discerning of spirits.

"And again, it is given to some to speak with tongues; and to another is given the interpretation of tongues.

"And all these gifts come from God, for the benefit of the children of God." (D&C 46:11–26.)

Since all have not every gift, but the gifts are to benefit all, we should not feel inadequate when we see that others possess gifts we have not experienced. We all have need of each other, and we each have some gifts and talents unique to us. Consequently, we can be of great service to others. In this way, we are all interdependent on each other. With this circumstance, we are all able to give and receive, and this process sanctifies us.

As we enter spiritual graduate school, we should not be concerned about the vehicle the Lord chooses to carry his instruction. Compared to the celestial knowledge, the vehicle is irrelevant. However, I bear you my witness that as we progress, we discover new talents and gifts, and this will continue as long as we dedicate them to blessing the lives of the Lord's children.

Epilogue

In the preface, I dedicated this book to the rank-and-file members of the Church—especially those who have not held the more visible positions in Church government and may be having some questions relative to their eternal progress. This group is on my mind partly because it is the group from which I came and partly because of the common expression I have heard from them: "I know the gospel is true, but I'm not sure I'm good enough or strong enough to make it." I pray my humble words have had some impact on your confidence and feelings of spiritual self-worth and that this confidence will lead you to a desire to keep climbing upward to new plateaus.

I would like to summarize all I have written by telling an experience of someone close to me who experienced the three plateaus in a short, three-year period. Another reason for sharing this is to reach out to those who have not for whatever reason seen fit to join the Saints in full fellowship. By this I mean specifically those who at this moment have not put aside whatever is keeping them from receiving their temple blessings. Sometimes we refer to these individuals as "less active."

Our approach to less-active members is not always as sensitive or loving as it could be. Perhaps I should use myself as an example because as an elders quorum president, I made some mistakes in this regard. When I was called, I decided to meet in the home of every member whether or not they attended any meetings. I had never met some of those brethren. On my first visit, after exchanges of pleasantries and gathering the family around, I would ask the prospective elder, "Don't you want to be with your family forever?" Now that sounded like a legitimate question to me at the time, but with hindsight I can see that asking a man or a woman that question in front of their spouse and children is very unfair. In fact, I would go so far as to say it was a "cheap shot." Of course, they want to be with their family forever, but at the current time there are conditions affecting that eventuality. This makes the question unanswerable. If the answer was yes, he knew I would jump all over him. If he said no, his wife and children would jump all over him. I asked the wrong question.

I sometimes catch myself asking my children "unanswerable" questions of the same sort. I will ask a son, "Do you want to break your neck?" Of course not, but he does want to climb on the garage roof. I will ask, "Do you want to starve to death?" Of course not, but he doesn't want to eat his big, squishy peas or lima beans either. I guess my favorite is, "Do you want a spanking?" Not once have I had a child answer, "Oh, please!"

Having repented of that approach, I would like to reach out to the less active by telling you about my Uncle Bill. His story crystallizes the progression of the plateaus from testimony, sanctification, and spiritual graduate school.

First, let me describe Bill to you. Everyone will recognize him and think I'm talking of someone they know before I get to the specifics. He was a big, strong man. When he shook my hand, my bones cracked. It was difficult for him to sit through long meetings and he couldn't stand to be in a suit and tie. He loved nature. He didn't like being assigned to visit someone. "If I want to visit, I'll visit." And yet, if someone was in trouble or needed help, he was there, unassigned. If the widow next door or across the street needed help, he was there. He could fix anything. However, after being married for fifty years, he still had not taken his wife and children to the temple.

When I received my current assignment on April 5, 1985, my favorite card of congratulations came from Uncle Bill:

> Glenn, I just wanted to tell ya how proud I am of ya. You should be proud too because you accomplished something nobody else has ever been able to do. You got this old reprobate of an uncle of yours to watch general conference. Bill. P.S. Yours was the best talk.

In July of that year, he and my Aunt Fon celebrated their fiftieth wedding anniversary. After the reception, I walked them out to the car and once more, Uncle Bill told me how proud he was of me. I replied, "Thanks, and do you know something else? With this call, I also received the sealing power. One of these days, if you'll bring Aunt Fon to the Salt Lake Temple, I'll tell you what I'll do for you. I'll perform your sealing for free!" They both gave nervous chuckles and a loving smile. I wonder what would have happened if I had said, "Uncle Bill, don't you want to be with Aunt Fon forever?"

Months passed and one Sunday evening I returned home at about midnight from a stake conference. There was a note from my wife where she knew I would find it — on the refrigerator door: Call your Uncle Bill, no matter what time you get home.

Even though it was late I took Bill at his word and returned the call. He told me that he had called to collect on the anniversary present I had given him. I put my hand over the telephone receiver and asked my wife, "What did we give Bill for his anniversary?"

Before she could answer he said, "You know, the free marriage sealing in the Salt Lake Temple."

I responded, "Are you serious?"

He said, "Yup, as a matter of fact the bishop is still here. Do you want to talk to him?" (He wouldn't let the bishop go home until I called.)

The bishop confirmed what Bill had said, that he was working toward getting his temple recommend. I asked Uncle Bill when they planned to go to the temple and he said, "The bishop thinks I can be good enough in two months."

This good man had been on the first plateau for years. I never questioned that he had a testimony and there was a lot of good done in his life because of his testimony and because of the fact that he was basically a very good man. He was now ready, however, to make a total commitment and go to the temple where he would receive the blessings that would put him well on his way to the second plateau of sanctification. There was already some of this taking place due to the trials he had suffered in his life as well as the service he had performed for others. But now a greater infusion of the Spirit would be possible because of this final commitment.

A date was set and there in the Salt Lake Temple, Uncle Bill and Aunt Fon were sealed to each other and to two of their middle-aged sons who had previously received their endowment.

A year passed and I received a phone call from one of his sons, my cousin, informing me that there had been a tragic accident. His nineteen-year-old daughter, who had been married about a year, had been killed in an automobile accident. He was at the hospital with her awaiting the arrival of his wife. He asked if I would come up to be with them. This I did and there participated in a very sobering and sacred event. I stood with my cousin and his wife over the lifeless body of their beloved daughter. I described this event earlier in this book. As we went to the viewing later in the week, Uncle Bill sought me out. He was very close to this granddaughter and he shared with me his great gratitude to his Father in Heaven that he had seen fit earlier to do those things which needed to be done to place him in complete harmony with the gospel. He said, "I don't know how I would ever have been able to stand this if I didn't know that I would be able to be with her again." He added, "As a matter of fact, I feel that when I go to the other side she will be allowed to usher me home."

On several other occasions he expressed his happiness and shared some very sacred experiences he had had relative to feeling the presence of those in the spirit world. He was encouraged and comforted at this particular time in his life. It was as if he had received a speeding-up of the sanctification process and he was definitely enrolled in graduate school.

Another year or two went by and I received another call from my cousin telling me that Uncle Bill was very ill and asking me to come to the hospital and administer to him. Priesthood leaders who have received similar calls will understand the humility and anxiety one feels at such an occasion. There is no time to prepare—except to pray for inspiration to say that which should be said.

I walked into the hospital and saw the family gathered around the bed and felt not only humility but inadequacy. There was my aunt who had faith in the Melchizedek Priesthood and in her nephew who was a General Authority. I looked into her pleading eyes and then went over to the bed and chatted with Bill, who was conscious and coherent at the time. I spent five minutes just stroking his beautiful white hair and then nodded to my cousin to join me in the blessing. As I placed my hands upon his head, I looked again into the pleading eyes of my aunt, but the impression that came to my mind as I sealed the anointing went something like this, "Bill, I bless you that the pain you have experienced will subside and that you will be able to spend the next few days having great joy and rejoicing in your posterity, and then you will begin to have a reunion with those who have passed on to the other side."

When we finished, I looked up expecting to see disappointment in my aunt's eyes but, although there were tears, she gave a knowing smile which told me the Spirit had borne witness to her that the blessing was the will of the Lord. Uncle Bill took hold of my hand. To my memory, it was the only time that we shook hands that he didn't crack my knuckles. He gave me a big smile, pulled me down to his head where I kissed him on the cheek, and he said, "Glenn, thanks for the anniversary present."

I don't know what Bill's final judgment would have been if he had not made the final commitment prior to his death. There is one thing, however, of which I am certain. The last three years of his life were the happiest of his life. He told me that on many occasions.

Too often we decide we had better start living the gospel in order that we can escape punishment on the other side. We need to realize that the joy of living the gospel is not postponed until after death. The benefits derived from following the Lord's plan are to be experienced now. We can receive much comfort prior to receiving the ultimate comfort of returning to the presence of our Father in Heaven. We can experience the joys of the sanctification process and marvel in the teachings of the spiritual graduate school.

If Bill were able to pen his own words, I'm sure he would say something like this, "Don't wait until you're seventy-five years old to put your life in order. I had no idea what I was missing."

I testify that we do not have to arrive at our destination before we can enjoy the fruits of the journey. By the Spirit of the Holy Ghost we can know with certainty that we are on the right path. We can know we are moving in the right direction prior to knowing we have arrived.

Index